What Media Classes Really Want to Discuss

You probably already have a clear idea of what a "discussion guide for students" is: a series of not-very-interesting questions at the end of a textbook chapter. Instead of triggering thought-provoking class discussion, all too often these guides are time-consuming and ineffective.

This is not that kind of discussion guide.

What Media Classes Really Want To Discuss focuses on topics that introductory textbooks generally ignore, although they are prominent in students' minds. Using approachable prose, this book will give students a more precise critical language to discuss "common sense" phenomena about media.

The book acknowledges that students begin introductory film and television courses thinking they already know a great deal about the subject. *What Media Classes Really Want to Discuss* provides students with a solid starting point for discussing their assumptions critically and encourages the reader to argue with the book, furthering the "discussion" on media in everyday life and in the classroom.

Greg M. Smith is Professor of Moving Image Studies in the Department of Communication at Georgia State University. Recent publications include *Beautiful TV: The Art and Argument of Ally McBeal* (2007) and *Film Structure and the Emotion System* (2003).

£14.99

What Media Classes Really Want to Discuss

Routledge
Taylor & Francis Group

LONDON AND NEW YORK

32302235419
LA236
(302.23) SMI

First published 2011
by Routledge
2 Park Square, Milton Park, Abingdon, Oxon, OX14 4RN

Simultaneously published in the USA and Canada
by Routledge
711 Third Avenue, New York, NY 10017 (8th Floor)

Routledge is an imprint of the Taylor & Francis Group, an informa business

Typeset in Sabon by Taylor & Francis Books
Printed and bound in Great Britain by
TJ International Ltd, Padstow, Cornwall

British Library Cataloguing in Publication Data
A catalogue record for this book is available from the British Library

Library of Congress Cataloging in Publication Data
Smith, Greg M., 1962–
What media classes really want to discuss : a student guide / Greg M. Smith.
p. cm.
1. Motion pictures. 2. Television broadcasting. I. Title.
PN1994.S575 2010
791.3071'2--dc22
2010005145

ISBN 13: 978-0-415-77811-4 (hbk)
ISBN 13: 978-0-415-77812-1 (pbk)
ISBN 13: 978-0-203-84642-1 (ebk)

To the teachers who really made a difference in my life:
Linda Quinn, Andy Whitwell, Ruth Day, Bobby Allen, Tom
Gunning, John Fiske and David Bordwell

Contents

Preface

A note to the student about why this book is different

You probably already have a clear idea of what a "discussion guide for students" is: a series of not-very-interesting questions at the end of a textbook chapter. Instead of triggering thought-provoking class discussion, all too often these guides lead to busy work for you.

This is not that kind of discussion guide.

This guide is different is because a film/television/media class is unlike many other introductory classes you may take. You have been immersed in media your whole life, and so you are already familiar with "realism" and "identification." You do not need to be introduced to media in the same way that an accounting student needs to learn what the "modified accelerated cost recovery system" is. You probably are already much more primed to talk about whether media cause violence rather than discussing your opinions on the correct method for calculating depreciation methods. Your preexisting knowledge is one reason why I am glad I teach media classes and not accounting, but this familiarity also presents difficulties. The concepts of "realism" and "identification" that have served you thus far are probably not precise enough to help you make clear points in class discussions. If everyone in class has a slightly different understanding of what "realism" is, then you may end up talking past each other. This guide seeks to provide you with a language that is a bit more nuanced than the commonsense terms you already know.

Chances are you already have thoughts about whether media cause violence or how films promote stereotypes. I also have positions on these questions because I have been wrangling with them for years in classes. You'll notice that I use that not-very-textbooky word "I." In this book I am not going to pretend that I have a "neutral" stance about these issues, and so this guide does not have a typical "textbook" tone. At times I will share rather personal insights from my life. (One quick note about writing style: This book tries to use an approachable tone, but your class instructor may want you to use a more scholarly way of arguing than I do. That's OK, since you are at the beginning of your studies. Trust me: It takes a lot of scholarly experience to learn to write simply and clearly.)

I consider myself to be intervening in a discussion that started long before this class and that will continue throughout your life. If you and I are going to wrangle over these matters, you need to have a clear position to argue against, and that is what this book provides. Instead of a series of "neutral" questions, this book presents essays where I lay out positions about key concepts. I believe that the concepts and arguments in this book will help you think more clearly about film, television, and media. I don't expect you to agree with all of these ideas, nor do I necessarily expect that your instructor will, either. I hope that you will *argue* with this book. If you do, then this book will have done its job in furthering the "discussion" on media in your life.

Chapter 1

"It's just a movie"
Why you should analyze film and television

The question arises almost every semester. My introductory media class and I will be hip deep in analyzing the details of a particular film, and then a hand will creep up, usually from the back: "Aren't we reading too much into this? After all, it's just a movie." Taking a deep breath, I then launch into a spirited defense of our analytic activity. After five or ten minutes of this, the student usually has a shell-shocked, what-did-I-do-to-deserve-this look on her face.

I've never been pleased with my spur-of-the-moment justifications of film and television analysis, which tend to come across as a bit defensive. Worst of all, they don't deal with the full complexity of the question, and I do believe that it is a very profound question. Why are we spending so much time finding new meanings in something as insignificant as a movie or a TV show? Aren't we just "reading into it?" The student's question deserves a fuller answer, or rather, it deserves several answers. As a way of finding those answers, this chapter extends the dialogue started by that series of brave, inquiring students in my classes.

Nothing left to chance

"All right, do you really think that every little thing in film and TV is there for a reason?"

Lots of things in our everyday world are there by accident. If I trip over a stone that causes me to bump into someone, that jostling encounter is probably not part of a higher design. It's just a random occurrence of the sort that happens all the time, with no enormous significance in the real world. There is a temptation to treat film and television in a similar manner, as if spontaneous things occur by chance. Nothing could be further from the truth.

Hollywood films and network television shows are some of the most highly scrutinized, carefully constructed, least random works imaginable. Of course, we know this, having read *Entertainment Weekly*. We all know that it takes thousands of people to create mainstream media: directors and actors, grips and gaffers. We know that producing film and television is a highly coordinated effort by dedicated professionals, but to most people it's a bit of a mystery what all these people do. When we watch film and television, we are encouraged to forget about all that mysterious collective labor. A movie usually asks us to get caught up in the story being told, in the world that has been created for us, not to be aware of the behind-the-scenes effort that brought us this story and this world. We tend to forget the thousands of minute decisions that consciously construct this artificial world.

When I put on a shirt in the morning, I do so with very little thought (as my students will tell you). A movie character's shirt is chosen by a professional whose sole job is to think about what kind of shirt this character would wear. Similar decisions are made for props, sound, cutting, and so on. Most mediamakers work hard to exclude the random from their fictional worlds. Sets are built so that the mediamaker can have absolute control over the environment. The crew spends a great deal of time and expense between shots adjusting the lighting so that each shot will look as polished as possible. When mediamakers want something to seem to be random, they carefully choreograph this random-appearing behavior. For instance, extras who are merely walking by the main characters are told where to go and what to do to appear "natural." Even seemingly random events and minute details in a film/television program are chosen and staged.

But what about directors who don't sanitize the set, who try to let bits of the real world into their work (from the Italian neorealists to Kevin Smith's *Clerks*)? What about actors, such as Dustin Hoffman and Robin Williams, who like to improvise? What about documentary mediamakers who don't script what happens in front of the camera? What about reality TV? Don't these let a little bit of chance creep into the film? Not really (we will talk further about this in Chapter 2). One could say that these strategies let some chance occurrences make it onto the raw footage. However, the mediamaker and the editor watch the collected footage over and over, deciding which portions of which takes they will assemble into the final cut. They do so with the same scrutiny that was applied to the actual shooting. Even if they recorded something unplanned, they make a conscious choice to use that chance occurrence. What was chance in the production becomes choice in the final editing.

Italian neorealism was a filmmaking movement that began in the physical and economic devastation of post-World War II Italy. Under these conditions the Italian film industry could not make films with the technical polish of their 1930s output, and so they turned their poverty into an advantage. Beginning with Roberto Rossellini's *Rome, Open City*, the Italian neorealists used real locations in war-torn Italy (instead of tightly controlled sets); available lighting (instead of nuanced theatrical light); nonprofessional actors (alongside trained professionals); and a looser, more episodic way of telling stories (instead of tightly controlled plotting). Italian neorealism strikingly contrasted with Hollywood's slick studio output, making these films seem more grounded in the details of real life. Although the movement was short lived (ending in the early 1950s, when Italy became more affluent), its influence was enormous. Many "new waves" of filmmaking hark back to neorealism as a way to distinguish their look from the Hollywood norm. Hollywood itself incorporated some of neorealism's features (location shooting, episodic storytelling) beginning in the 1950s to give its films a more realistic feel. Key figures in the movement include Rossellini, Vittorio De Sica (*Bicycle Thieves, Umberto D*), and screenwriter/theorist Cesare Zavattini.

"Come on, do directors, editors, and set designers *really* spend all that time scrutinizing such details?" Think of it this way. A Hollywood blockbuster may cost up to $300 million. If you were to make something that costs that much, wouldn't you examine every tiny detail? Even a "low budget" film can cost $30 million or so. With so much money riding on a film, the scrutiny is enormous, and it extends to all levels. Of course this process, like all human effort, is fallible; mistakes do sometimes creep in (for example, an extra in *Spartacus*—set in ancient Rome—can be seen wearing a wristwatch). All too often, beginning media scholars have a tendency to assume that odd moments in the film/television program are mistakes, when the opposite assumption is more likely to be true. Nothing in a final film or television episode is there without having been examined by scores of professionals who have carefully chosen the components. You can trust that if something is in a movie, it's there for a reason.

A movie is not a telegram

"Okay, so the director really cares about the details. But do you think your interpretation is what she really meant to say?"

In high school English classes you may have been taught to look for the meaning of a literary work, a single sentence that summarizes what the author was trying to convey. So you might have boiled Shakespeare's *Macbeth* down to a single sentence that reveals the moral lesson to be learned from the play (perhaps "Greed for power corrupts people"). One can reduce a literary work or film or television program to its message, which makes the game of interpretation a fairly simple one. All we have to do is figure out what the author/director was trying to say.

Some mediamakers have scoffed at the idea that their work contains any such messages. Hollywood producer Samuel Goldwyn is alleged to have said, "If I wanted to send a message, I would've called Western Union" (the nineteenth/twentieth-century equivalent of text messaging). What is at issue here is the conception of what communication is. The traditional understanding of speech considers a sender trying to relay a message to a receiver (often called the S–M–R model). A sender has a clear intention regarding what she wants to get across to the receiver, but she may not present her message particularly clearly. The receiver tries to understand the message, but she can misunderstand the sender for a variety of reasons. By comparing the sender's intention with the receiver's understanding, one can discover how effective the communication was. For example, if a receiver gets a text message asking for bail money and then starts collecting the necessary cash a successful instance of communication has taken place.

The *sender–message–receiver (S–M–R) model* was proposed in 1949 by Claude Shannon and Warren Weaver as an outgrowth of their work with telephone companies to improve the accuracy/understanding of phone conversations. It has been expanded to become perhaps the most dominant framework for understanding communication. A more fully elaborated S–M–R model also includes an awareness that the channel/medium affects the overall communication; that there is "noise" on that channel that can interfere with the message; and that the receiver/audiences can communicate "feedback" to give the sender a sense of whether the message is getting through. Theorists have proposed numerous elaborations and expansions on the S–M–R model, but it still remains at its core a fairly one-way model of linear communication.

It is tempting to conceptualize film and television as communication in this way. To see how effective a movie is, one could compare the mediamaker's intentions with our interpretations and see if we "got it."

If the audience member didn't receive the message, then perhaps the movie is poorly made or perhaps the viewer is not very savvy.

Films, television shows, plays, and novels, however, are not telegrams or cell phone text messages; they are infinitely more complicated. One of the first traps that the budding critic should avoid is thinking that a film or TV program can be understood as having a single message which we either "get" or not. To do so is to treat it like a telegram. Cinema and television are richer forms of communication than can be conceptualized as sender–message–receiver.

"Okay, so perhaps the director isn't just sending a single message. Maybe she's sending several messages. If we can figure out what those messages are, then we've got it, yes?"

First of all, there's a big question concerning who the "author" of a film or television program is. Thousands of people put their work into a major media project. If all of them are trying to convey meaning, do we have to consider all their combined intentions? Or if some people's contributions are more important than others (actors, directors, cinematographers, producers), then can we understand a movie as the sum total of their intentions? The question of authorship in film and television is a much thornier one than the question of a book's authorship.

Let's make it easy on ourselves. Let's assume that the author of a movie is the person who is in charge of coordinating all decisions in the shooting process: the director.[1] If we can figure out what the director intends, then we've got it, right? If we could interview Hitchcock and gain an understanding of what was going through his mind when he made *Vertigo*, then we would have gained a pretty solid hold on the film, yes?

But can we reduce the film to what the director consciously intends? At times we all express the beliefs, attitudes, and assumptions of our era without necessarily being conscious of doing so. Did Hitchcock fully understand his attitude toward blonde women, or was he propagating a widely held belief in his society? Sometimes the ideology of our day speaks through us with little awareness on our part. In addition, we can unconsciously express personal issues as well as social attitudes. Many believe that the unconscious seeks to express painful things that we have repressed and buried within ourselves. These tensions can emerge

---

1 In film and television, the director is usually in charge of the process of shooting, though she may not be in overall control of the final product. In some films the producer has the right to the "final cut." In most television shows, the director of an individual episode is hired by the person in charge of the overall series, called the "show runner." In this situation, the director answers to the show runner.

in our everyday lives through dreams or Freudian slips or the artwork that we make. Perhaps Hitchcock was unconsciously working through his own personal obsession with cool, aloof women in ways that he did not even understand as he made *Vertigo*. Since human beings cannot be reduced to their conscious thoughts, films should not be reduced to the director's conscious intentions.

"Okay, okay, so if we get a sense of what the director's conscious intentions are, what ideological beliefs she gained from her socialization, and what her unconscious issues are (admittedly a difficult process), then we've arrived at a well-grounded, comprehensive description of what the movie is trying to communicate, right?"

We have, if we stay within the sender–message–receiver model that works for text messaging. But let's step outside that model. Why should we limit the viewer to making only those meanings which come directly from the sender/mediamaker? If I get meaning from media and apply it to my life, why should I have to check with the mediamaker to see if that's the right meaning? In other words, why should the mediamaker have more authority over interpreting the film/television program than I do?

"Because she's the director. It's her movie," you may reply. I would respond, "You're the audience. It's your movie, too." If you let go of the notion of a mediamaker trying to convey a message, then the audience's activity is to interpret the film according to their lives, their experiences, their tastes—not the director's. That activity is just as valid as the mediamaker's. A movie's meaning does not lie solely within the film itself but in the interaction of the film and the audience.

As we learn more and more about how audiences interpret media, we discover what a striking range of interpretations people make. If we consider those interpretations to be somehow less valid than the mediamaker's, then we lose much of the complexity of how media work, make meaning, and give pleasure in our society.

"Reading into" the movie

"But those audiences are just reading things into the movie, right?"

Let's think about what "reading into" a movie is. "That's simple," you might reply. "It's when an audience puts things into the movie that aren't there." That certainly seems straightforward enough. But is it?

Picture yourself watching a horror movie in which a group of teenagers are staying at a spooky cabin deep in the woods. It's midnight. A couple sneak off to a back bedroom and have sex. The attractive young woman then gets up, decides that she's going to take a shower, and says that she'll be right back.

You know that this woman will be toast in a matter of minutes.

But how do you know? There's nothing in the film itself which says that this woman will die. The same incident (romantic rural location, sexy couple) could take place in a romantic comedy, and the shower would not raise any hackles. No, the knowledge of her imminent death comes from you, the experienced horror film viewer. You have "read into" the scene.

Like the characters in *Scream*, you know that horror operates according to a set of rules or conventions that have been established by previous members of the genre. The mediamaker depends on you knowing these conventions. She knows that by sending the woman to the shower, she can create tension in the audience. ("No! Don't go, you crazy girl!" Hopefully you don't advise your real-life friends not to shower.) The filmmaker can toy with the audience, delaying the inevitable, because she knows that we expect the girl to be slashed. It is our job as audience members to read into the scene; mediamakers count on that.

Film and television rely on the audience to supply information that is only hinted at, like the shower convention in horror. This "reading into" even occurs at the simplest levels of mediamaking. When we see a shot of someone getting into a car and driving away, followed by a shot of the car pulling into another driveway, we understand that the driver drove from one place to another. We understand this without the film/TV show actually showing us the drive across town. If we were limited to what was explicitly laid out in the TV program, if we didn't read into the film, then we wouldn't be able to make basic sense out of them. There's not a choice of whether you read into film/television or not; audiences have to.

This is not to say that you can read media in any way you want. Certain pieces of information in a film/television show are established beyond dispute. If you don't think that *Seinfeld* is about friends hanging out in New York City, then you have missed something. If you believe that it is a television series about Arctic beekeeping, then you are doing a remarkably perverse bit of reading into.

Between the pedestrian kind of reading into (the driving-across-town example, which some would call an inference or expectation) and the ludicrous kind of reading into (*Seinfeld*-as-Arctic-beekeeping) there is a wide range of possible readings. Some of these you may find to be too much of a stretch. What I would ask is that you be open to the possibility that some of these readings may be interesting. Don't close down your mind simply because an interpretation involves "reading into" a movie, because all media viewing involves reading into. Instead, look at the film/television program with an open mind and see if there is evidence to support a particular interpretation. If someone says that *Seinfeld* is really about the search for God or about Freudian revenge on the father, look at the TV show to see if there is corroborating material. Based on the film/television program, decide if there is a case to be made for that particular interpretation.

Just a movie

"Okay, maybe I see the value of coming up with new interpretations of *Hamlet* or *Citizen Kane*, but *Seinfeld*? *Evil Dead 2*? *Rush Hour*? *Everybody Loves Raymond*? *Survivor*? Come on. Aren't you taking these a bit too seriously? After all, it's just a movie (or a TV show)."

You wouldn't say, "Why are you analyzing *Hamlet*? After all, it's just Shakespeare." Why is it okay to analyze Shakespeare and not *Evil Dead 2* or *Everybody Loves Raymond*? The answer has as much to do with the social status of these works as it does with the works themselves.

There was a time when the study of Shakespeare would have been questionable as being not serious enough. At first, scholars in the West didn't think that anything written in English was as worthy of study as the classics written in Greek. Homer, Sophocles, and Aristotle were the serious works which should be taught in school, not Shakespeare's plays or Dickens's novels. Lawrence Levine has traced how the status of Shakespeare's work has changed in America, from a rather lowbrow standing in vaudeville productions to its current highbrow connotation as Art-with-a-capital-A. Dickens's novels, now clearly considered classics, were serialized in newspapers as pulp fiction. In that day, to argue that Dickens's work should be taught in schools would have seemed almost scandalous. Such trash obviously could not withstand the scrutiny applied to great works like Homer's *Odyssey*, or so it must have seemed.

Instead of relying purely on our society's understanding of what kinds of artworks are good enough to be taken seriously, we should instead look to the artworks themselves. If we look for rich interpretations of a work, we may find them or we may not. The point is not to dismiss the process outright simply because it's "just a movie." The proof is in the pudding, as the old saying goes. If your analysis produces insightful, well-grounded interpretations of a film/TV program, then that media text is definitely fruitful for analyzing, even if it is titled something like *Evil Dead 2*.

No one will argue that all media works are equally rich for analysis. Probably *Hamlet* is a more complex text to examine than *Evil Dead 2* is. But that shouldn't lead us to neglect a text that is "just a movie" or "just a TV show." You should take insight where you can get it.

And even if a certain media text is not particularly complex, it can still provide hints about the society that produced it. Events don't have to be overtly complicated to yield knowledge.

For example, Robert Darnton, in his essay "Workers Revolt: The Great Cat Massacre of the Rue Saint-Séverin," analyzes a particularly unpromising-sounding phenomenon: a mock trial and execution of some cats by the apprentices and journeymen in a Parisian printing shop in the 1730s. What could this bizarre, sadistic, and unusual ritual possibly tell us about French society of that time? Reading closely, Darnton shows how this odd ceremony can reveal much about the relationship between workers and bosses, the sexual and class structures of the society, and the tradition of a craft. His essay demonstrates that even the slightest cultural artifacts bear the imprint of the society that made them. Examining a film or television program can give us clues about the meanings and assumptions that are shared by the members of a culture. If a mock trial of cats can reveal social interrelationships, then an uncomplicated film/TV show that doesn't bear much aesthetic scrutiny can be examined for its social insights. All cultural products carry cultural meaning.

Ruining the movie

Part of the resistance to applying analytic tools to *Evil Dead 2* or *Survivor* is the belief that such analysis will kill the pleasure we have in watching them. After all, movies and television are intended to be "mere entertainment." We have already dealt with the question of the media-maker's intention, so let's not deal further with whether or not we should be limited to the mediamaker's conception of their work as "mere entertainment." Instead, let's deal with the fear that analyzing a film or television program will destroy the simple pleasure of watching it.

Sometimes it seems that the surest way to ruin a good book is to have to read it for a class. English classes are supposed to make you read things that you wouldn't normally pick up yourself. They force you to read Chaucer or Joyce, and the process of analyzing these works hopefully gives you insight into your life. But that's a very different thing from reading Michael Crichton or John Grisham in the airport. There you're reading to escape. If we start thinking too hard about airport novels or mainstream films, doesn't it ruin them?

When people learn that I am a media studies academic, they frequently ask, "Are you ever able to just sit back and enjoy a movie, or are you always analyzing it?" The question never rings true to me because it's phrased as an either/or option. For me, it's not a matter of substituting cerebral analysis for visceral pleasure; I experience both simultaneously. I don't lose the pleasure of rooting for the good guy while I'm admiring a movie's editing and thinking about the plot's social ramifications. After taking media studies classes, I can add the pleasures of analysis to the pleasures of moviegoing and television viewing.

I realize that as you are taking an introductory media analysis class, it may not seem like there's much pleasure in analysis. It probably seems more like tedious, difficult work. At first it may seem that you're losing the pleasurable experience of film and television as you dissect them, but as you get better at analysis, you will be able to recombine those activities. The end result, I believe, is a richer kind of pleasure. I believe that I respond more fully to movies and television than I did before I started analyzing them. I now feel joy at a well-composed shot, a tautly constructed narrative structure, and an innovative social commentary, as well as the simpler pleasure of finding out whodunnit. The outcome we hope for in a media analysis class is not to ruin film and television but to increase the complexity of your enjoyment.

Why do that? Why tinker with the simple pleasure of watching a movie? This question goes to the foundation of what education is. The basic faith underlying education is that an examined life is better, richer, fuller than an unexamined life. How do we really know that self-examination is better than the bliss of simple ignorance? Like most statements of faith, there's no way to prove it. But by being in a college classroom, you have allied yourself with those of us who believe that if you don't examine the forces in your life, you will become subject to them. You can go throughout your life merely responding to movies and television, but if you are an educated person, you will also think about them, about what they mean and how they are constructed. In so doing, you may gain pleasures and insights that you could not have obtained any other way. This is the promise of the educated life in reading, in living, and in watching.

An earlier version of this chapter appeared as "It's Just a Movie: A Teaching Essay for Introductory Media Classes" in *Cinema Journal* 41.1 (Fall 2001): 127–34.

Bibliography

Darnton, R. (1985) "Workers Revolt: The Great Cat Massacre of the Rue Saint-Séverin," in *The Great Cat Massacre and Other Episodes in French Cultural History*, New York: Random House.

Levine, L. (1990) *Highbrow/Lowbrow: The Emergence of a Cultural Hierarchy in America*, Cambridge, MA: Harvard University Press.

Part 1

Discussing how media work

Chapter 2

What is realism, really?

Realism initially appears to be a straightforward concept, and yet people use this single word to describe a dizzying array of media. When I ask my students to list films and television programs that they consider to be realistic, I elicit an enormous range of suggestions, including animation (such as *King of the Hill*), sitcoms (*The Office*), reality television (from *Jackass* to *The Apprentice*), Oscar-winning blockbusters (*Saving Private Ryan*), low budget independent fiction films (*Paranormal Activity*), "based on a true story" TV movies, 24-hour news channels (CNN), and documentaries (from *Animal Planet* to *Capturing the Friedmans*). How can all these different programs be "realistic" in the same way? What can "realism" possibly mean if applies to all these different media?

Like many commonsense words we will cover in this book, "realism" needs to be broken down into more precise terms if the concept is going to give you insight into film and television programs. Understanding realism better is not simply a matter of learning new terminology. This chapter will pay attention to the different nuances of what we mean by "realism." Behind those shades of meaning, various assumptions are lurking concerning the relationship between media and the real world. This chapter articulates those multiple assumptions so that you can examine them more closely.

Here at the beginning of the chapter, I will ask you to set aside the loosest way to think about realism. To judge whether a media text is realistic, it would seem obvious to compare the film/television program with reality. Simple enough, yes? And yet I would argue that film and television always end up on the losing side of that comparison. If you compare any film or television program to "reality" (however you define that elusive concept), the media are always found lacking. Film and television always condense. An event that unfolds over hours, days, or even years gets compressed into a 90-minute documentary, and a film "based on a true story" may merge several real-life people into a single character. Mediamakers select which things to include, which necessarily means they also leave things out. Even filmmakers who pay strict attention to historical details cannot possibly hope to capture the full range of everyone's experience of even one significant event. Reality occurs 24 hours a day with an enormous "cast" of characters, each with his/her own perceptions. There is no way that film and television can compare favorably to the breadth, depth, and complexity of the real world.

And so I believe that a simple comparison between film/television and reality is not very useful because it always arrives at the same conclusion: media simplify (or "distort") the truth about the real world. I wish to move our discussion past the notion of whether a film or television program is telling the "truth." Instead I will discuss realism as a set of techniques that mediamakers can choose to adopt. What these techniques do is encourage us to *believe* that the media are being truthful. This is not exactly the same as "telling the truth" (if such a thing is possible), but it is a powerful effect that both fiction and nonfiction mediamakers can aspire to achieve. We can recognize when television feels "true to its subject," even if the television program is fictional, and that recognition changes the way we think and feel about the media text. Of course, no film or television program has total power to convince everyone that it is realistic. Individual viewers may raise doubts, and no media can fully override or anticipate this. But certain techniques tend to encourage our belief in the medium's realism, and these techniques are part of the toolkit available to every mediamaker. Realism is not "natural"; it is something people *do*.

In this chapter I will argue that it is useful to think of realism as being composed of many different things, not just a single concept. Although we use the same word to describe a wide range of media, realism comes in many forms, constructed by a mediamaker's techniques, interpreted by audiences based on their assumptions. There are many realisms.

The many forms of realism are variations and recombinations of two broad trends that John Caughie calls the "dramatic look" and the "documentary look" of realism. The "dramatic look" of realism is what you know as the "invisible" Hollywood style. The goal is to get you involved in the characters' lives without becoming too aware of the filmmaking process, whether in a standard sitcom or in a made-for-TV movie. The camera and editing work together seamlessly to give the audience a clear view of any important story moment. The dramatic look offers us the pleasure of being an invisible observer eavesdropping on another world. Our expectations about the "documentary look" of realism, on the other hand, have developed from watching documentaries where a limited number of cameras capture events that often cannot be repeated (if you are capturing a real-life riot on video, it's hard to yell "Cut!" and ask the rioters to do it again). Unpredictable occurrences make it difficult for documentary mediamakers to convey events with the clarity of the dramatic look. The documentary look is not as smooth as the dramatic look, but it captures more of a visceral pleasure of "being there." These two "looks" (one developed in fiction filmmaking, the other developed in nonfiction) are now familiar enough that they can be used in either fiction or documentary mediamaking. They are two broad "flavors" of realism, but (as we will see) they are composed of multiple components that can be mixed into a variety of concoctions that we still recognize as "realisms."

Apparent spontaneity

Our understanding of realism is often guided by a broad assumption that reality is not pretty. Any content can potentially be captured in a realistic manner, but we generally do not picture high tea in a formal English garden when we discuss realism. If a Hollywood fiction film shot with the dramatic look is considered to be particularly realistic, it often is set in a less-than-glamorous world. There is a bias in what we generally think of as realistic content toward the gritty, the untidy, the lower class. This is not because we think that aristocrats are not real or that beautiful objects do not exist, but there is a long history of realism being used to expose harsh conditions that we need to reform in the world. This historical link remains powerful in the way we think about the very nature of what is realistic. It inclines realistic media toward the unpolished, both in terms of their content and their style. The documentary look is particularly associated with a style that appears messier, less controlled, and less planned. Let us look at several ways that a realistic style can call upon this assumption that reality is messy.

Some forms of realism depend on an *apparent spontaneity*, either in the world we see and hear onscreen or in the way that world is captured. Our expectation of spontaneity depends on an assumption that "reality" is relatively unplanned. Although you may plan what you are going to do during the day (what you will wear, where you will go, and so on), you probably do not control your life with the level of detail of most Hollywood feature films. You do not script your lines in advance, nor do you rehearse your friends, family, and colleagues until your interactions are smooth and polished. Realism often depends on conveying this same sense that people are "making it up as they go along."

Of course much that happens in the real world is highly scripted. When the President of the United States addresses the nation, his every word is carefully constructed; the lighting, setting, and camera position are crafted; every piece of clothing is chosen, every hair styled into place. This does not make the President's speech less "real" (in fact, the President's address is scripted because every word can have real, serious consequences). This does mean, however, that you probably didn't think of a Presidential address when you were thinking of "realistic" texts because there is so little spontaneity in these speeches. There is more apparent spontaneity in a press conference with reporters or an election debate or a "town hall" meeting with ordinary citizens, though these scenarios are different blends of spontaneity and preplanning. Again, it is useful to think of these media situations not in black-and-white terms ("realistic" or "not realistic") but as different combinations of realistic strategies. The President appears to be less in control of the give-and-take of a town hall meeting with ordinary people than of a professional interchange with reporters, and so we watch and listen to such media events in hopes that we will catch a glimpse of what the "real" (unvarnished) President thinks.

The word "apparent" is just as important to our understanding of this aspect of realism as the word "spontaneous" is. We do not have the inside information to evaluate whether a political event is truly spontaneous. Apparently ordinary citizens stepping to the microphone may deliver a scripted question, or the President can insert well-rehearsed sound bites into his seemingly off-the-cuff answers. Politically-minded citizens seek behind-the-scenes information that helps them discriminate what's really going on, but that doesn't change the basic mechanism of realism. If a relatively uninformed person believes that the interaction being shown is relatively spontaneous, it will seem more realistic to him. The same is true for someone who knows more about politics. If a particular political moment comes across as being less rehearsed (satisfying the more rigorous standards of someone who knows political stagecraft), then even a hardened political vet will tend to think of such moments as "realistic."

As in many of the examples we will discuss, realism occurs when there is a match between what the individual assumes and what the mediamaker does. What the individual knows varies from person to person, and it varies from film to film depending on the filmmaker's choices. But it is not an entirely individual phenomenon, either. There are reliable patterns in realistic media based on broadly held assumptions about how media are made. These assumptions, such as the expectation of assumed spontaneity, have certain prejudices. A filmmaker can reliably use techniques that call on these assumptions, that nudge us imperfectly toward believing in the realism of what we see/hear.

Apparent spontaneity (based on the assumption that the real world is messy and unorganized) takes multiple forms. Sometimes spontaneity is primarily *visual*, as in the use of *loosely framed compositions*. A loosely framed shot does not try to look "perfect." It does not arrange objects to be symmetrical; the composition can be off balance, and people/objects move in and out of the frame freely. One of the ways that the show *Cops* signals that it is unstaged is by showing us intentionally sloppy camerawork. The camera operators hired by the show are proficient professionals who are fully capable of nicely framing shots of the perpetrators once they are captured, shots that are well balanced and perfectly composed. Such shots would call attention to themselves by their "artsy" quality, and so *Cops* videographers avoid such framings so that the show will appear less artificial. We accept such careful compositions as part of the dramatic look of realism, but the documentary look tends toward more casual compositions.

Filmmakers using the documentary look often make certain that the world doesn't look too manicured. Instead of using the system of glamour lighting that Hollywood has developed to ensure that its beautiful stars look their best, the documentary look tends to emphasize *"available" lighting*, the kind of light found in everyday situations. Of course many independent filmmakers cannot afford the labor-intensive process of carefully lighting each shot to perfection, but the choice of using available light is not a purely economic one. Shooting with what appears to be standard fluorescent or incandescent light has esthetic consequences as well. We read the image as being less carefully managed, even if the seemingly "natural" light is actually highly manipulated by the professional filmmakers. Because we associate this lighting style with the documentary look, this technique becomes available for fiction filmmakers who want to create a rougher, more worn world than the sleeker realism of the dramatic look.

A *jerky or handheld camera* has become another visual hallmark of the documentary look, particularly when that camera reacts to the action rather than anticipates it. Consider the moment at the beginning of every episode of *The Price Is Right* where contestants are selected from the audience to "come on down." The camera swoops erratically across the crowd, looking for the location of the screaming person whose name has been called. This is exciting partly because it appears visually spontaneous. The camera operator seemingly does not know where the lucky person is sitting, which visually reinforces the notion that this person has been randomly chosen from among the prospective players. But of course this is a realistic effect; employees from the show interview people waiting in line to enter the studio, selecting those who match the characteristics they desire on Contestant's Row. It would be simple enough to alert the camera operator to where the next contestant is sitting, but to help disguise this lack of spontaneity in choosing players, the camera operator jerks the camera around to "find" the right person.

Contrast this with the editing and camerawork in a sitcom such as *Everybody Loves Raymond*. After one actor delivers his/her line, the camera cuts to the person whose turn it is to speak next, and so on. Unlike a real-life conversation, the mediamakers know in advance when the characters will speak, and so the camera anticipates by perfectly framing the next speaker to deliver his/her line. This is a perfectly acceptable technique in the dramatic look of realism; however, the documentary look frequently relies on a *reactive camera*. "Direct cinema" filmmakers such as David and Albert Maysles (*Salesman*, *Grey Gardens*) and Frederick Wiseman (*High School*, *Near Death*) attempt to give us a "fly-on-the-wall" perspective on the world they are investigating, swinging the camera back and forth when someone begins to speak. Fiction mediamakers can use this same technique to give a more realistic sense of an *ER* or of the future (*Children of Men*), even when the filmmakers know who will speak next.

> *Direct cinema* is a school of American documentary filmmaking that is closely related to the French "cinema verité" (cinema truth) approach. These approaches to nonfiction filmmaking were a reaction to previous documentary work that used a "voice of God" (recorded in postproduction) to comment on what was being shown. The direct cinema filmmakers believed they could capture a more authentic, less preachy version of the world. The movement's handheld camera style is associated with lightweight cameras and synchronized sound recording on location. Both of these technical innovations enabled the direct cinema filmmakers to use small crews, permitting them to take a more intimate approach to their subject. Other key filmmakers in the direct cinema/cinema verité movement include Robert Drew, D.A. Pennebaker, Richard Leacock, Jean Rouch, and Barbara Kopple.

Not all realism relies on unbalanced framing or a reactive, handheld camera or available lighting. In fact, some documentaries set out to emphasize the beauty of the world (*Glass*, *Berlin: Symphony of a City*). But documentaries and fiction films that use seemingly sloppy techniques depend on our expectation that a realistically presented world will be visually spontaneous.

We have a similar expectation that the "documentary look" will also involve "documentary listening"; in other words, the universe will be more *verbally spontaneous* as well. It is acceptable for the dramatic look to show us classically staged dialogue scenes with characters enunciating clearly and taking turns exchanging well-crafted lines. (My ex-wife said she could recognize when I was watching a 1930s or 1940s era film in the next room simply by listening to the rhythms of the crisply articulate speech.) The overall effect can be elegant, as if the characters were passing a conversational baton back and forth. The more that a film leans toward the documentary look, the more it tends to break up that rhythm. Ordinary speech tends to be much more fragmentary. People interrupt each other; they talk over each other's words instead of waiting for their turn. They halt, not knowing quite how to phrase what they want to say, and they start again. We assume that real conversation, like real space, is messy.

Fiction filmmakers have been working to integrate more realistic forms of acting and delivering lines since the early 1910s, with perhaps the most significant change coming in the 1950s, when actors began to adopt variations on Stanislavsky's "Method." This approach, which asked actors to use vivid personal memories to give their performances an emotional truth, was seen as a revolutionary new way of grounding fiction in the real world. And yet if you look back at the great "realistic" performances of the 1950s (or any previous era), they sound mannered. This helps us see that "realism" is always a moving target. The realism of one era can sound stylized in another. The conversations in *On the Waterfront* or *Pulp Fiction* can sound more like poetry to our ears than realistic discussions about a washed-up boxer's dreams or a Quarter Pounder in France. We hear these conversations differently not so much because the world has changed but because filmmakers have developed other techniques that we understand to be "realistic." Each one of these techniques was designed to sound realistic at a particular moment in media history, and so as the practice of media making changes over time, so does our understanding of realism. So when Elia Kazan's actors stop speaking in crisp diction in the 1950s (*On the Waterfront*), or when John Cassavetes encourages his actors to improvise dialogue in the 1960s (*Faces*), or when Robert Altman begins recording overlapping dialogue between his characters in the 1970s (*Nashville*), or when sound mixing becomes lusher and denser in the 1980s, each of these strategies changes our expectations for how fictional realism might sound.

Constantin Stanislavsky (1863–1938) was one of the founders of the Moscow Art Theater. His writings and teaching have become the modern foundation for naturalistic acting in film, television, and theater. Stanislavsky created a system for how actors should prepare for roles, which involved (among other things) using personal memories of emotions and sensations to help them create emotions onstage. The actor should break down the role into a series of objectives (statements of what the character wants at a given moment) and then combine these with his/her own personal memories to create a psychologically realistic character. Stanislavsky's work became more widely popularized by American teachers (Stella Adler, Lee Strasberg, Uta Hagen) who formalized his thought into what is known as "Method acting."

Improvisation is an important verbally spontaneous strategy for many mediamakers. Some filmmakers do not like the "canned" feeling of dialogue where the actors know what line is going to come next, and so they use improvisation to give a looser feel to the conversations. Mediamakers can integrate improvisation into different portions of the production process, giving them varying degrees of control. Some filmmakers use improvisation during rehearsal to create a scene whose lines feel natural to the actors, but then they script a repeatable scene out of this material that they can capture in multiple takes. Others allow improvisation to happen while the cameras are running, although that can leave the editor with fewer options when piecing a scene together. The television comedy *Scrubs* encourages its actors to improvise their lines on camera, which has the added benefit of keeping the performances fresh when actors have been playing the same role for eight years. Fiction mediamakers (such as Mike Leigh) and nonfiction documentarians (Jean Rouch) have a faith that audience can somehow sense the difference between scripted and improvised interaction, even if once-improvised lines are repeated in separate takes. They believe that incorporating improvisation into production yields a kind of truth that cannot be arrived at through the most honest and forthright script.

A third form of apparent spontaneity (*narrative spontaneity*) has to do with the construction of the story itself. We have grown to expect that a tautly constructed film will leave out the "boring stuff," that it will only show us events that are narratively significant. If such a film shows us a scene of a mundane activity (taking a shower, for instance), we assume that something dramatic will happen (a horrific attack by a serial killer, perhaps). Of course millions of people in real life take showers with no expectations of being stabbed; the real world is not as tightly plotted as a Hollywood blockbuster; everyday life rarely has the on-the-edge-of-your-seat quality of an action film. Some mediamakers believe if a film only includes events that are absolutely crucial to the plot's forward direction, this does violence to the film's sense of being in the real world. If a filmmaker aims for a breathless pace, this may suck the real life out of the film. To this way of thinking, real life is what happens in between the big moments.

Take, for instance, *Bicycle Thieves*, a 1948 Italian film about a father and son trying to recover a stolen bicycle that is the source of their livelihood. In the middle of their search, they drop by a restaurant, have a meal, and chat. Of course anyone in the real world has to eat, but imagine this happening in a pulse-pounding big budget thriller. Try to picture John McClane in *Die Hard* stopping off for a burger and fries before he continues his rescue mission. Doing so would create a very different fictional world, one where digressions are just as important as pursuing goals.

Italian neorealist films (such as *Bicycle Thieves*; see Chapter 1) made popular many of the apparently spontaneous techniques we are discussing here (from available lighting to a more easygoing approach to storytelling). These influential films helped open up the possibilities for "slice-of-life" films, ranging from loosely structured "road trip" films (from *Easy Rider* to *Little Miss Sunshine*) to films focusing on the interactions in a particular place and time (from *The Last Picture Show* to *Barbershop*). The pleasure of these films is in "hanging out" with the characters, not in rushing to save the day.

Once these slice-of-life films showed a less plot-intensive way of depicting the world, this innovation was taken up by a wide range of mediamakers, even those who create big budget event films. One of my favorite scenes in that classic Hollywood blockbuster *Jaws* has almost nothing to do with hunting the shark. Quint, Brody, and Hooper drunkenly participate in a macho storytelling competition, comparing tales about their injuries (both physical and emotional). At the end of this scene, they all sing "Show Me the Way to Go Home." One could easily excise this scene without endangering the plot about tracking down the killer shark, but this little digression both gives us a bit of breathing room in the harried plot and lets us know more about the characters' backstory. It gives a lovely human moment in the middle of the monster movie.

I am not arguing that *Jaws* is a remarkably realistic film (the shark still looks fake), but this moment feels more "real" to me, not because this scene feels improvised (it is tightly scripted) or because of any apparent visual spontaneity. This scene is recognizable to me as an ordinary activity: hanging out, sharing stories. I recognize that this scene is just as fictional and staged as the shark attacks, but this conversation comes across as being more realistic because it is not so tightly woven into the fabric of the story. In the overall story structure, it feels more "spontaneous."

Filmmaker Steven Spielberg could have pushed the realism of this moment further by adding more apparent spontaneity (messier compositions, improvised dialogue). Overall he could have added more off-the-cuff moments such as this one if he wanted *Jaws* to have more of a realist feel. Each mediamaker can choose to deploy various realistic techniques, and mingling these techniques helps give a particular text its "flavor." For instance, what we call "reality television" is a mix of various realistic devices. *Survivor* is not particularly narratively spontaneous; it pre-scripts a series of artificial challenges for its contestants, leading up to a "tribal council." We assume, however, that the contestants' actions and reactions while participating in these contests are not preplanned. We recognize that people speaking directly to the camera may not be particularly "true to life," but their halting, sometimes inarticulate speech makes these moments feel verbally unscripted. *Survivor* at times shows us gorgeous compositions of tropical vistas, but when following individuals in mid-competition it avoids such artfulness.

A broad label such as "reality television" may confuse as much as it enlightens. There is much realism in *Survivor* or *The Real World* and much that is clearly not realistic. Paying attention to various specific techniques (such as the various forms of apparent spontaneity) helps us discuss more clearly what is realistic about such shows.

The interpretive frame

We have learned the principles of visual, verbal, and narrative spontaneity partly from interacting with the real world and partly from watching film and television. We judge a character's awkward, ungrammatical speech as being more realistic because his/her dialogue does not sound like the rhythms of more typically scripted media. Our expectations are shaped by our previous film and TV experiences.

Some of these expectations become standardized over time. Because we have seen many documentary films and television programs, we have learned to associate certain established strategies with the "language" of documentary. For instance, we readily recognize "the interview," a setup where one person asks questions and another answers. Once we label a situation as an interview, this triggers a particular set of assumptions about how to judge what we see and hear. In this section I will focus less on the details of how a filmmaker handles a situation and more on the power of the situation. Once we recognize these standard setups, they serve as a *frame* that encourages us to interpret the material inside that frame as being more realistic. The label itself can exert a powerful realistic effect.

Consider the phrase "based on a true story" that appears at the beginning of many films. These simple words ask us to interpret the film differently. What we see and hear may follow a typical Hollywood fiction formula: a determined young man earns his chance to play college football (*Rudy*), or a portrait of war as hell (*Glory*). It may present well-known actors delivering clearly scripted lines. But that phrase "based on a true story" asks us to have a certain level of faith that goes beyond the dramatic realism of fiction filmmaking. Although we expect that the filmmakers may have fudged some of the details (simplifying events, putting words into people's mouths), this phrase asks us to trust that the film is essentially faithful to the key points of the story. Of course there is little way for an audience to tell exactly which portions of the dramatic realism are indeed "based on a true story," and so the film asks us to extend a certain level of belief across the whole film. Although both *Seabiscuit* and *The Black Stallion* are well acted, dramatically scripted, lushly detailed, visually beautiful portraits of horse racing with exciting Hollywood climaxes, we are asked to interpret *Seabiscuit*'s based-on-a-true-story narrative as being more realistic than *The Black Stallion*'s, though at times they look much alike. A film that declares its true-world origins may not have to work quite as hard visually to convey a sense of realism. For instance, *We Are Marshall* is shot with a fairly standard "dramatic look," assuming that the historic tale of a college football tragedy will help us believe in its realism, no matter how unlikely its events are. An entirely fictionalized depiction of American football such as *Any Given Sunday* may have to use jerky cameras and overlapping, fragmentary dialogue to convey a sense of realism. When we know that a film has real-life source material, this knowledge frames the way we make sense out of the film, even if the film uses the dramatic look much more than the documentary look.

Sometimes the interpretive frame involves knowing who the media-makers are. A film or television program can gain a sense of believability based on our previous experiences with the the program or its makers. A segment on *60 Minutes* gains a certain amount of authority simply because it airs on a program that has a longtime reputation for jour-nalistic excellence. We have a kind of *journalistic contract* with the makers of a well-respected news show that they will make a good faith effort at presenting a version of the "truth." Standards of journalism vary, so one person's trusted source may be another person's biased mouthpiece. Regardless of whether the source is Fox News or PBS, once that trust is established with a viewer, this adds to the realistic force what we see and hear on these programs. Again, my focus here is not on the individual report itself (which may vary in how closely it sticks to the truth) but on the realistic force of the context. Simply by being on a trusted news program, the report gains in authority because we trust that the content has passed high journalistic standards.

Even fiction films can gain a realistic effect if we trust the filmmaker's knowledge about the subject. When Spike Lee sets a film in the Bedford Stuyvesant neighborhood of New York, I assume that he is getting the details right, since he is portraying an area he knows intimately. Since I do not have much knowledge about Iranian culture, I trust filmmaker Majid Majidi's greater understanding of Iranian village life in *The Color of Paradise*. This aspect of media realism is an outgrowth of one of the oldest concepts in rhetoric. *Ethos* is the Greek term for the persuasive power of a speech that is due solely to the speaker's characteristics. We listen differently to a woman talking about abortion than we do to a man. We tend to trust a doctor's health advice more than our neighbor's, though they may be giving the same advice. We factor in what we know about the speaker/filmmaker when we assign truth value to words and images. Even if the words and images are exactly the same, we interpret them differently once we know something about their source.

For example, Forrest Carter's *The Education of Little Tree* is a charming, seemingly autobiographical book describing a boy's upbringing by his Cherokee grandparents. It was taught as part of American Indian literature/culture courses until it was revealed that "Forrest Carter" was actually Asa Earl Carter, a Ku Klux Klansman who wrote Gov. George Wallace's famous "segregation today, segregation tomorrow, segregation forever" speech. The words on the printed page are still the same, but it is hard to read this book with the same sense of realism that one has when reading it as a memoir. Although the novel still has many realistic techniques, the frame for interpreting it has changed. It no longer is subtitled "A True Story" on the cover, and the subtitle makes a difference, even if nothing else is changed.

We may have specific knowledge of how a film or video was made, and that knowledge can give the media a sense of realism. Knowing that amateur photographer Abraham Zapruder was in Dallas at the time of John F. Kennedy's assassination helps give his 26-second recording the status of legal evidence. Although few people knew the filmmakers of

The Blair Witch Project, those who allegedly thought the footage was indeed shot by doomed filmmakers would give the film a strong sense of realism. Again, the point is not whether any particular piece of footage is "real" or "fake." Even a "fake" can be considered realistic if it encourages us to think it is true to life. Knowing about the mediamakers or about the specific circumstances of a recording can help us frame the media as realistic (from a YouTube clip to a national news story).

Realism as recording

Our knowledge about media, then, is a crucial component of why we believe certain media are realistic, which André Bazin (the most influential theorist of film realism) understood. Bazin believed that film and photography (and television) by their very nature are considered more realistic than other arts such as painting and sculpture. We accept these media as being able to capture reality because of what we know about how they work. We know that once you turn on a camera it captures what is in front of it without the camera operator having to do anything else. Organizations install surveillance cameras because they trust these machines to give an unadulterated depiction of what happens in a space. No one questions the idea that a video recording could give more accurate "testimony" than an eyewitness, and no other medium is given this same level of trust. Imagine if a poet or painter had seen the Los Angeles police beat Rodney King in 1991, and they tried to enter a poem or painting as evidence in court! The other arts require the artist to intervene at every moment when trying to record an event. For a painter to capture a vase of flowers on canvas, he/she must recreate by hand every petal, every marking on the vase. Each paint stroke creates the opportunity to alter the image in ways that are clearly "subjective." There is nothing "automatic" about the process.

> *Rodney King* (born 1965) became nationally recognized when his 1991 arrest by Los Angeles police officers was captured on a widely circulated video. The footage showed white policemen beating King (an African American) with batons while he was on the ground. The officers were acquitted of charges related to police brutality in a high profile trial, sparking an outburst of race rioting.

Good films and photographs are obviously not automatic, of course. There is considerable artistic intervention in choosing where to place the camera, how to arrange things in front of the lens, and so on. And yet our basic knowledge about filmmaking helps us accept that once the film and television camera starts recording it will capture what is in front of the lens both automatically and accurately. This property makes it easier for film and television to attain a basic realism, while a painter must work hard to achieve a similar accuracy.

Of course this belief in film's and television's ability to capture what is in front of the lens is a kind of faith, as Bazin noted. Because of what we know about cameras, we believe that film and television are capable of being faithful to the world. Because of what we know about editing, we also understand how filmmakers can rearrange footage to "lie" about an event. We bring our faith and our doubt with us when we watch the simplest of scenes.

Take, for example, a scene in which a highly paid actor appears to fall down the stairs. If the scene shows us a panicked closeup of the famous actor's face atop the stairs, then cuts to a body falling down the stairs who keeps his face away from the camera, followed by a shot of the actor's face as he sprawls at the bottom of the stairs, we all know what happened in the filming of this scene. We know that the big budget film did not want to endanger the expensive star, so they had a stunt person take the tumble down the stairs, and they intercut the two actions to look relatively continuous. Although we accept this "cheat" as fairly standard Hollywood procedure, in this small moment we understand that the basic faith in capturing action has been violated. Although we may still care about the danger that the character is in, our sense of that danger lessens because we do not believe it in quite the same way.

Now consider an alternative in which we see the actor take the tumble in one long, continuous shot. Bazin would say that this scene takes advantage of the film medium's fundamental realism. Although we still understand that this is a film about a fictional character, we also understand that the same actual flesh-and-blood person who has been playing that character had to take that painful spill down the stairs. Because of what we know about filmmaking, we easily make judgments about how realistic that fall was.

Filmmakers differ in how much they emphasize the fundamental realism of film/television. For example, consider the movie *Grindhouse*, which is actually two films, one by Robert Rodriguez (*Planet Terror*) and one by Quentin Tarantino (*Death Proof*). One way to think about this film is that it stages an argument between Rodriguez and Tarantino about whether realistic action or special effects is the most exciting. Rodriguez's film is full of special effects, from explosions to artificial limbs that fire machinegun bullets. Tarantino's *Death Proof* takes an alternate approach, staging a car chase where the character Zoe Bell is hanging onto the hood of a car with her bare hands. The camera emphasizes that the actual woman is holding onto an actual car as it careers down the road (it helps that the character is played by stunt woman Zoe Bell). You probably have your own preference on which is more exciting: special effects or captured live action. But there is clearly a distinctive thrill to watching a Jackie Chan film, knowing that Chan is doing his own dangerous stunts (which he emphasizes by showing us outtakes—including his injuries—during the closing credits). As Bazin said, directors can use film techniques to preserve and extend the realism that cameras capture automatically. That realism exists partly in the film and partly in our minds because it relies on our basic understanding of how filmmaking works.

Much has changed since Bazin wrote about realism in the 1940s. Some would say that we no longer have the same kind of faith in the camera's ability to capture reality in our intensely Photoshopped world. One could argue that every time we look at a photo that appears in our email inbox nowadays, we doubt that picture's reality more than we believe it. Did that cute kitty really touch the lion's face, or were two pictures merged using software? I would once again emphasize that so much depends on what we know about how the picture was taken. I do not believe that we have totally lost faith in the camera's ability to capture the world accurately. We no longer take anonymous images at face value (if we ever did). But I still believe that a picture of an atrocity taken by a reputable source can still move people to outrage. I believe that Bazin is still right. If our knowledge about how the image was taken confirms that the image is trustworthy, we can still believe in the image's fundamental realism, even in this highly technological era.

As our image technology changes, it becomes apparent that the cinema's fundamental realism is actually composed of several components. Film's realism partly depends on the *density of picture information* that comes by exposing light to film. There are painters who paint in a photo-realistic style, attempting to duplicate the density of film, but such art takes an incredible amount of time, compared to the detail captured automatically in film. There is much more information in a film frame than in a single "frame" of traditional television, which gives film an advantage in capturing spaces with a sense of lush detail (one way that television compensated for its relative lack of image density was to emphasize its ability to *broadcast live*, which film cannot). With high definition television (HDTV), the medium now can deliver approximately the same picture density as film. Digital games also struggle with the relative lack of density in their images. Rendering a game space in detail takes considerable computer time and processing power, and still the images on a computer game do not look quite like reality. The objects in a computer game are shinier because it is easier for computer generated imagery to create slick surfaces rather than the rough hewn texture of the real world. Digital games compensate for this relative lack of realism by giving players a more "interactive" experience, allowing us to explore the space more freely than film and television can.

Bringing up computer games reminds us of just how important it is to break "realism" down into components. The digital gaming industry is constantly pursuing a more information-packed image, with each new game platform increasing the hardware's capacity to render space in detail. When game designers discuss the desire to make games more "realistic," they are not usually implying that strategies of world conquest or infinite supplies of ammunition are true to life. They mean that they want to increase the technological capacity of the hardware and software so that digital "people" look more like real people. They want to build on one particular aspect of the complex concept of "realism."

The *level of detail in the picture* itself also varies, with consequences for the realistic effect. If the space being shown is packed with objects and textures, this can feel more realistic to us. The difference here is not in how much picture information there is in a frame (each frame of HDTV has the same number of pixels); the distinction is in how many details are placed in that frame.

Details have historically been important to realism, even in its written forms. A realistic novel often depends on lush description of place and character to give a strong sense of "being there." Getting those details right is crucial to creating a convincing setting. Again, there is an assumption here, that if a fiction writer or mediamaker takes care with the minutiae, we should trust that other aspects of the story are true to life. This is not an assumption that necessarily makes logical sense, but it is an important part of realism. Mediamakers take incredible pains to make sure that the sets and costumes are right for the specific setting for their story. To show how much effort filmmakers spend on detail, let me cite my favorite credit line of all time, found in *The Age of Innocence* (Martin Scorsese's adaptation of the Edith Wharton novel about 1870s' New York society). As the closing credits roll, you will notice that they hired a "cutlery consultant." Was Martin Scorsese concerned that people would stand up in the middle of his film and shout, "Fraud! That is an 1865 soup spoon, not an 1872!" I doubt it. But I would wager that Scorsese was deeply concerned with making sure the set "felt" like a realistic reproduction of the time and place. Although few of us have the kind of expertise required to judge the period cutlery, we can sense that lavish attention has been paid to the set, even down to the place settings at the table. If the details feel right, this encourages us to generalize our faith to broader issues. Perhaps, then, we can more easily trust that Scorsese is correct about the aristocratic manners or the sexual politics of the era. One form of realism can contribute to another.

When Hollywood retrenched in the 1950s to produce fewer films, it made sure that each film received intense attention to the production values. In the 1930s and 1940s, if a filmmaker wanted to show a boy's room it was usually enough to put a "Princeton" pennant on the wall. After Hollywood reorganized to focus its efforts on each individual film, this lack of detail was no longer enough. Fast-forward several decades to *Boogie Nights*, to the 360-degree pan showing us Eddie's room, where every inch is covered with posters. This space is not generic; it is intensely particular and personal. A set designer/dresser has chosen each one of these decorations with Eddie's character in mind, and so this densely packed space feels like where Eddie lives. Hollywood today ensures that the spaces in a big budget film are intricately constructed to give even fantastic worlds a sense of realism. Although we have no way of knowing what a "real" Death Star would look like, we would expect that its surface would be richly textured, as all the spaceships in *Star Wars* are (one of the groundbreaking aspects of *Star Wars* is how detailed the futuristic gadgetry is). And so we can talk about futuristic fictional worlds as being "realistic" if the mediamakers have packed detail into the image.

When I hear undergraduates say, "I don't like old black-and-white films," I think that they are partly responding to the relative lack of detail placed into the image (and the soundtrack) in films of the 1930s and 1940s, rather than the lack of color. The spaces in a typical blockbuster today are more filled with objects and sounds, giving us more to look at and listen to. Capturing details gives a dense sense of realism to the world that the camera records.

Plausibility and consistency

Throughout this chapter I have been emphasizing that realism involves more than just a simple comparison between media and the real world. I do not want to entirely divorce realism from our experience of reality, however. Sometimes our knowledge of the real world does have an impact on whether we think a particular film is realistic.

Sometimes a film violates our *general sense of how the world works*. If a hero makes it through a violent skirmish while maintaining perfectly styled hair, or if terrorists enter government buildings without encountering security guards, or an earthquake exposes exactly the right cave where the treasure is buried, or if an unemployed actor can afford a spacious Manhattan apartment, these events can trigger your internal plausibility alarm. The real world doesn't operate like this, we say. Real hair gets ruffled; security guards are not that careless; earthquakes do not make searching easier; and rent in New York City is expensive. These circumstances only happen in the movies, we recognize. If mediamakers do not provide justifications for these situations (super hair spray; bribed guards; an ancient prophecy; a rich family), then these implausibles can kick us out of the story. Notice the word "can" in the previous sentence. Not everyone notices such story implausibilities, and it is the filmmaker's job to draw our attention away from such thoughts. If a film does trigger such real-world objections in an individual, however, the film's sense of realism is (at least temporarily) broken.

A character's actions can go against our general understanding of what "human nature" is. If a character does not react strongly enough to the death of a beloved friend, or if people forgive others too lightly, or if characters accept the hero's return without question after a long disappearance, this can jeopardize our belief in these characters' realism. "People just don't act like that," we say to ourselves, "at least not the people I know," and we blame the acting, the script, or the directing for ejecting us from the film's world. I recall having one of these general plausibility crises while watching Steven Spielberg's adaptation of *The Color Purple*. Timid Celie has to be taught by the bold Sofia to want to fight back against her abusive husband. When I saw the film for the first time, I thought that this simply did not ring true. I could certainly believe that an abused wife would be afraid to confront her brutal husband, but I could not accept that such a person wouldn't even want to oppose him. It was utterly outside my experience to think that anyone could be so abused that they didn't desire retribution for their oppressor. Years later, however, while working at a crisis call center, I did encounter such real-life women in abusive relationships, and it changed my understanding.

Celie's reaction seems much more plausible to me now, given what I know about people like her. Realism depends on our conception of how "people like that" act, think, and feel. We carry with us a whole set of templates for how certain types of people interact with the world. This understanding of specific character tendencies helps simplify the world as we move through it. It helps to be able to predict how abused wives, lawyers, Christians, mothers, bullies, drug addicts, and spoiled brats will act. If a film shows us a bully's sudden change of heart or a lawyer accepting a client whose trial begins the next day, this can interrupt our sense of the film's realism. A film can justify such actions by giving specific motivations to these characters (giving the bully a romantic crush on a pacifist girl, or making the lawyer's client a long-lost buddy), and each of us evaluates whether these motivations make sense, given what we know about these characters and about people like them. Murray Smith says that films encourage us to simulate a character's actions mentally. We ask ourselves, "If I were that character—if I had the same experiences, beliefs, and attitudes—would I behave like that?" If we answer, "Yes," then the film gains a sense of *specific character plausibility*.

Plausibility in character action is closely related to our expectations of consistency. We expect that people do not do things randomly; they tend to act in similar ways unless important forces change their lives. Dramatic realism is based on an assumption that the world is a consistent place. We accept that different fictional worlds may behave according to different rules, but we expect the fictional universe to play within those rules once they are established. Even fantastic universes need to function with consistency if we are to accept them. We don't particularly care what laws govern how magic or time travel or superheroes or monsters work, as long as the film does not violate those restrictions. A zombie film like *28 Days Later* situates its fantastic elements within a world that is otherwise recognizable to us. It encourages us to ask, "If you can accept a world where zombies exist, then how would that world work realistically?" It may seem strange to talk about a "realistic" monster movie or superhero film, but many filmmakers believe that their fantastic creations will be more exciting if they operate in an *internally consistent universe* (in other words, a world that resembles our own world).

If a zombie suddenly heals much faster than it previously did (just in time for the climactic battle), then we suspect that the filmmaker has manipulated the world to make the story work out. We sense the filmmaker's hand reaching from outside the world of the film into the realistic world he/she created. This intervention reminds us that this is a work created by people and not an independent world.

Of course we already know that a film is something created by humans, but dramatic realism wants to deemphasize that awareness, to immerse us in the world of the film. In one sense, dramatic realism is "lying" about what it is doing. What film actors are doing is actually quite artificial: they are speaking well-rehearsed lines and pretending not to see the extremely bright lights, the boom microphone, and the camera. Dramatic realism depends on a fiction: that we are eavesdropping on these characters without them acknowledging our presence (or the presence of the camera that gives us our view into this world). We accept this "lie" as an automatic part of realistic filmmaking, just as theater audiences accept the idea of a living room having only three walls (so that we can see into that room through an invisible "fourth wall").

Some filmmakers believe that it would be more "honest" to acknowledge the reality of the filming process instead of pretending that the camera and technical personnel did not exist. Consider a bedroom scene in a dramatic film. The filmmaker usually wants you to concentrate on the two lovers and their "natural" interactions within the fictional world. They usually want to hide what is actually happening: that many real people are crowded in that room, all engaged in highly "unnatural" activities (directing, acting, capturing sound and image). A truly "realistic" film would acknowledge that this is a movie, not a real bedroom interaction.

This more radical alternative to dramatic realism is called *reflexivity*, which is when a storyteller overtly acknowledges the process of storytelling and/or the audience as part of the story. A reflexive film reminds us that this is a film, a product created by workers for presentation to an audience, not a realistic world. Reflexivity tends to interrupt the consistent world of the film, interjecting reminders that we are not simply eavesdropping on a self-enclosed world. Reflexivity occurs when characters "break the fourth wall" to speak/look directly at us. This violates one of the earliest rules developed in film acting: "Don't look at the camera." This rule was crucial for the illusion of dramatic realism because a look at the camera acknowledged that the camera exists in the same world as the characters. When Groucho Marx speaks to us in asides in *Duck Soup* or when Ferris Bueller instructs us on how to get a day off from school by faking illness, they are acknowledging the existence of the usually invisible audience of onlookers. Reflexivity comes in many forms other than direct address. When the finale of *Blazing Saddles* reveals that the movie is being shot on a studio lot, or characters on the Fox TV show *The Simpsons* poke fun at the quality of Fox programming, or when the subject of a documentary attacks the camera, we can no longer pretend that the camera is our unseen emissary into a free-standing world.

This reflexivity is realism of a different sort; it problematizes notions of realism by emphasizing how artificial this realism actually is. It tends to interrupt the consistent world created by Hollywood films designed to deliver a linear story or by standard documentaries aiming to present a straightforward version of the truth, and so it acts against some of the realist forms we have been discussing. Admittedly, reflexivity sometimes feels like the opposite of realism. In a fiction film, reflexivity comes across as an acknowledgment of how fake filmmaking truly is. In documentary, reflexivity can remind us that the people being filmed are very aware of the camera. By calling attention to the constructed nature of realism, a reflexive moment can destroy the realistic illusion created by the rest of the film. Juxtaposing one form of realism with another makes us aware of just how much realism can vary as a style.

In closing, our belief in the film's realism varies from moment to moment. An interpretive frame can lead us to make initial assumptions about a film's realism, but then we monitor the film and adjust our judgment of its realism. Some moments trigger our realism monitoring very slightly, as in the example of the Hollywood star appearing to fall down the steps. Other moments may alter our understanding of the film's realism more radically, as in character implausibilities or reflexivity. Instead of making a simple decision whether a film is realistic or not, we constantly reevaluate the film's realism as the film continues.

Realism is not an "is it or isn't it" concept. A realistic effect depends on a match of viewer knowledge and media technique. Mediamakers rely on dependable techniques (verbal and visual spontaneity, for instance) and assumptions (plausibility and consistency) that encourage us to believe in the truth of the worlds they depict, whether those universes are fictional or nonfictional. These techniques depend on what we know about the world and about how films are made. Some of this knowledge is broadly shared (how cameras capture images automatically, for example), and some information used in making judgment (details about historic cutlery) varies greatly from individual to individual. Therefore individuals may disagree about whether a particular media text is realistic, but still there are broad patterns in how realism is constructed.

Realism, therefore, is not a simple comparison with the world. It is not a mirror we hold up to the world. It is a lens, and there is no such thing as a perfect lens. Think about when you used a magnifying glass as a child. By positioning the lens properly, you could make certain portions of an object come into sharp focus, while other parts went blurry. Every lens distorts the world in particular ways, and every form of realism does this as well. Just because realism distorts does not mean that it is invalid. Realism (like a magnifying glass) can shed useful perspective on things we would not otherwise see. Just as lenses do, realism can help us see faraway places that we otherwise would not know, and it can encourage us to see the familiar world around us with new eyes. Understanding the multi-faceted lens of realism may not help you decide if a particular image is ultimately, truly, absolutely real, but knowing how the multiple forms of realism work will help you understand how such images make appeals to our hearts and minds.

Bibliography

Bazin, A. (1967) *What Is Cinema?* vol. 1, Hugh Gray (trans.), Berkeley: University of California Press.

——. (1971) *What Is Cinema?*, vol. 2, Hugh Gray (trans.), Berkeley: University of California Press.

Caughie, J. (1981) "Progressive Television and Documentary Drama," in T. Bennett, S. Boyd-Bowman, C. Mercer, and J. Woollacott (eds.) *Popular Television and Film*, London: BFI Publishing.

Smith, M. (1995) *Engaging Characters: Fiction, Emotion, and the Cinema*, Oxford: Oxford University Press.

Further reading

Grant, B.K. and Sloniowski, J. (1998) *Documenting the Documentary: Close Readings of Documentary Film and Video*, Detroit: Wayne State University Press.

Hill, A. (2005) *Reality TV: Factual Entertainment and Television Audiences*, New York: Routledge.

Nichols, B. (1991) *Representing Reality: Issues and Concepts in Documentary*, Bloomington: Indiana University Press.

——. (2001) *Introduction to Documentary*, Bloomington: Indiana University Press.

Plantinga, C. (1997) *Rhetoric and Representation in Nonfiction Film*, Cambridge: Cambridge University Press.

Chapter 3

How do we identify with characters?

Films and television programs offer many pleasures. They focus on what is dramatically important, filtering out the boring parts (on TV, classes are always more interesting without those pesky, long-winded lectures). Media present the fantasy that we can always be where the "action" is, and that those important actions will be perfectly visible and legible to us. They can show us exotic lands (from Tatooine to Transylvania) in lush realistic detail, allowing us to "escape" while remaining in the comfort of our chairs. We can simulate experiences (being chased or being adored) without risking any actual danger or taking any responsibility for what happens. Movies and television programs can involve us in well-told stories that make us wonder what will happen next, and we get pleasure when our expectations are partly confirmed and partly denied.[1]

Media also offer us the pleasure of imagining what it would be like to be someone else for a while. With the aid of the onscreen images and sounds, we can vividly picture what it might feel like to be more powerful, sexier, smarter, and braver than we suspect we really are. We can assume the perspective of someone who is less fortunate, allowing us to feel pity or outrage at injustice without having actually to suffer injustice directly. Movies and television programs can help us extend our perspectives outside the limits of our own lives. They can mix wish fulfillment with realism (see Chapter 2) in various combinations to provide dependable, relatively low cost and low risk emotional experiences of "being in someone else's shoes." They offer us the pleasure of "identification."

Like many of the terms used in this book, people use the word "identification" in many different ways. I have heard people say that

---

1 If the plot is totally predictable we get bored, but if the story takes an entirely random twist we become frustrated.

they identify with the world of the film, or with a particular situation in a television program, or with the camera. Are all of these "identification" in the same way that we refer to "identifying with a character?" And what does "identifying with a character" mean? Does it imply something more than "caring for" a character? Does identification mean that we feel what the characters appear to feel? Then what about situations where we clearly care about the characters but we feel something very *different* from them (when we know that our beloved heroes are about to be attacked, but they remain calm and clueless)? People often use "identification" and "point-of-view" interchangeably, but do we identify with every character who gets a brief point-of-view shot in a movie? We all have experienced the pleasure of "identifying with a character," but what is identification, really? How does it work? And one last question ...

Why does identification matter?

Some media forms create strongly emotional experiences without offering us characters for identification. Take the circus, for instance. When you see an acrobat bounce off a springboard and land atop a pyramid of people, you may "ooh" and "ahh" at the spectacular achievement without particularly identifying with the circus performer. You may care briefly about the person's safety, but the circus is not designed for you to get too caught up in that individual's story, since it will move on to another performer's daring feat. Any "identification" you might have with the acrobat is fairly brief, although your momentary emotions can be intense enough to cause you to scream.

Consider how differently a movie about a circus acrobat might work (*Man on Wire*, a film about tightrope walker Philippe Petit, for example). We would learn the story of this particular circus performer, how he grew up wanting to master his art, the obstacles he overcame, his specific dreams, fears, motivations, and doubts. The film would encourage us to picture what it might be like to risk injury, to have perfect control of the body's muscles, to receive cheers and applause. Using visual techniques (showing us point-of-view shots) and storytelling devices (interviews with the performer and his friends), film encourages us to do more than marvel at the acrobat's skill (as we might do at the circus). The circus rarely gives us the same kind of backstory that makes the acrobat into an individual character with particular motivations and hardships. We assume that the circus performer must have dreams and obstacles, but we do not have much specific information about them, nor is it easy for us to see things from the acrobat's perspective atop the human pyramid. Any identification we might have with the acrobat at the circus is probably limited, since the circus focuses more on spectacle than story.

Or consider the pleasures of seeing a good exhibit of abstract art. You can marvel at the use of color and line, but it is difficult to picture yourself in the composition. You might identify with the painter of these artworks, but there is little in the paintings themselves that encourages you to picture yourself as the artist. Now consider a film or TV biography of such an artist (the movie *Pollock*, for example). The film offers you the opportunity to imagine yourself as swarthy, successful, arrogant, innovative, insensitive genius Jackson Pollock. We get the chance to feel what it might be like to splash bold color onto large canvases, and so identification in this biopic offers a different pleasure than looking at these artworks in a museum. Although identification is not necessary for us to have intense emotions in art, film and television usually offer us the pleasure of identifying with their protagonists and envisioning what it might feel like if *we* were that particular artist or that specific daredevil.

Identification's prominence in film/TV/gaming helps explain why our society is so concerned with images in those media. Mainstream film/ television/gaming seem to call for our participation. The characters they present are not "distant" from us like an abstract painting on a wall. These media seem to invite us to "try on" another person's perspective. One reason we seem to care about images of women (or African Americans or gays/lesbians) in television/film is because identification asks us to place ourselves in those positions. Only a rare museum exhibit rouses broad, angry criticism of its images in the same way we attack bad "role models" in film and television.[2] Although certain gallery artworks can encourage strong identification, the contemporary museum tends not to emphasize identification as much as present-day film, television, and computer games do. Although some were outraged by Andres Serrano's photograph entitled *Piss Christ* (which immersed a crucifix in urine), they objected because a social/religious taboo had

---

2 Of course this is a broad generalization with notable exceptions. Galleries also are more localized than film and television, which are mass media that are viewed internationally. Modern art is a less popular form than mainstream film/TV; it tends to attract a narrower, more educated audience; and gallery art is often considered to be relatively "highbrow." All of these factors influence the ways that museums cause different controversies from popular media.

been violated, not because they identified with the Christ figure in the artwork.

Andres Serrano's (born 1950) photography tends to deal with unsettling and shocking subjects (from corpses to body fluids). His work became notorious outside of gallery circles when his *Piss Christ* was denounced in 1989 by conservative senators who were outraged that the work had received funding from the National Endowment for the Arts.

In mainstream film and television, on the other hand, identification is a central lure for audiences, and so media scholars began to focus on identification partly because they recognized that we needed to understand how media images encourage us to care about characters. If we kept film and television images at a distance, they wouldn't matter so much to us. It is not enough to understand images of women, African Americans, and so on as if they were something separate from "us." (See Chapter 6 for a discussion of how the media portray "others.") We also need to understand how film and television encourage us to participate personally in those images. Film and television characters are not simply creations of directors, writers, and producers; we also help bring these characters to life when we lend a bit of our own selves to those figures onscreen. This is the power and the importance of identification.

The spectator

Media scholars turned to psychoanalytic theory as a way to understand identification, arguing that our earliest experiences of identifying with our parents/caregivers exert a powerful influence on all subsequent identifications with other people in the real world and onscreen. Such scholarship focused on the notion of the "*spectator*," which is a theoretical position that we have to occupy (metaphorically speaking) in order to make sense of and get pleasure from a film. Let's talk a bit about what scholars mean by this concept.

In order to make sense out of a film, according to psychoanalytic critic Christian Metz, we first need to "*identify with the camera*." We need to recognize that each shot is taken from a particular camera position, that the camera looks upward at the characters in some shots (called "low angles") and down at them in others (called "high angles"). Although we do not usually see the camera in the shot, we have to understand roughly where the camera is positioned if we are going to make sense out of the space we see onscreen. If we couldn't recognize the camera's position in relation to the action, then we would see the images as lines and colors in a frame (like an abstract painting) rather than people and objects in a space. Metz calls this process "*primary identification*" because it happens first. If we did not first situate our visual viewpoint in the film's space, we could not possibly identify with characters in that space. Without that orientation, we would not be able to recognize at the most basic level what the film was showing us.

Thus a film "repositions us" from shot to shot, a process so automatic that most of us are unaware that it happens. Of course, *you* don't actually move; you stay in your theater seat (hopefully!). In order to make basic sense of the stream of images onscreen, you must understand that your "position" changes whenever the camera changes. The position created by a film would be impossible to occupy in real life. At times we float above the action, then suddenly we are below it. We move close, then instantly we are far away. We may shift quickly from continent to continent or planet to planet, from the dinosaur age to a nuclear apocalypse. Film and television offer us the fantasy of being in the right place at the right time, unconstrained by distance, history, or the limits of our own bodies. And so you should not think of the "spectator" as a literal position. It is not a specific seat in the movie theater. Instead, it is a theoretical "position" that each film constructs differently, shot by shot. Each film encourages us to "occupy" that position in order to make sense of the images it shows.

Films and television programs want us to do more than just comprehend the onscreen action; they want us to feel emotions about what we see. In order to get an emotional payoff from a film or TV program, we have to occupy a certain position in relation to the story. Let's take a simple example. Imagine a shot that begins on a woman's bare legs and travels slowly up her body, lingering on her hips, moving up her torso to arrive at her perfectly lit face. At the most basic level, this shot simply asks us to label: "That's a woman." This shot also asks you to make certain assumptions about that woman. Based on our long experience with film and television, we know that this shot is asking us to see this woman as desirable. If we are going to get full enjoyment from the film, we need to feel her desirability instead of keeping her at a distance. Regardless of whether you are attracted to women (or whether you are attracted to this particular woman), this shot encourages you to feel attracted to her. It cannot force you to be attracted, but if you reject her desirability you are denying yourself the full pleasure that the film offers. You are not occupying the spectator position.

As this brief example shows, film mixes both visual and storytelling techniques to establish a spectator position. The film provides a series of shots, but it is the spectator's job to connect them mentally into a coherent story. A good film/TV program encourages us to predict what might happen later in the story, and our anticipation fuels our curiosity, propelling us forward. If we are immersed in a movie, it may feel as if the film is unrolling before our eyes with little effort on our part, but a film requires us to provide the connective tissue that links the shots and story together. The pleasure of being immersed in another world awaits anyone who occupies the spectator position, and whenever we go to the movies we hope that we will have a seemingly seamless ride.

Character identification plays a crucial role in placing us in the spectator position. The classical Hollywood cinema gives us at least one central character who is our emissary to the world of the film. In some films (from *The Wizard of Oz* to *Twilight*) this protagonist is a newcomer to the strange land, which conveniently requires that the inhabitants introduce themselves to the character (and to us) and provide explanations of how the world works. In detective films and television procedurals, we tend to receive information at the same time that the investigators do. We see the same things (as the camera follows our heroes) and hear the same dialogue, which encourages us to place ourselves closer to the protagonist's position in the story, to ask similar questions and make similar judgments.

Film and television programs often give their protagonists certain reliable qualities that encourage us to identify with them. They show us that the characters are good at what they do, or they place their characters in threatening situations. Television series can count on the added advantage of our previous identifications with its characters. Because we have a history of identifying with the same characters (sometimes over a period of decades), TV series do not need to spend much time reintroducing their cast and making us care about them. New episodes can assume that we are already allied with the beloved characters, and so they can immediately begin introducing guest stars or setting up this particular episode's dilemma.

If a film or television program can get us to identify with its characters, then this makes the spectator position appear more "natural." Characters don't have to explain the onscreen world directly to us; we simply overhear the dialogue. If the film/television program shows us an image that might make us uncomfortable, then it can reduce that discomfort using character identification. Let's return to that simple shot of the camera traveling up the attractive woman's body. Often such shots will be justified as some character's point-of-view, which means that we do not have to feel like a dirty voyeur who is "checking the woman out." After all, that's not *our* choice of how to view the woman's body. *We* are not being sexist; that's the *character*'s perspective. We are just along for the ride, which gives us a built-in defense against the charge of voyeurism. But remember that spectator positioning encourages us to participate in the story world instead of keeping it distant. The entire storytelling system encourages us to lend a portion of our thoughts and emotions to important characters, so in some sense *we* are also "checking the woman out" when we identify with the looker. By coordinating the camera's gaze with the character's gaze, this also powerfully controls the audience's gaze, offering us the pleasure of looking without seeming to give us responsibility for our emotions and thoughts.

Film theorist Laura Mulvey points out that our history of identifying with film characters in such situations is not gender neutral. In fact, because we have identified so often with male characters looking at female characters, the camera's gaze has itself become gendered. Mulvey notes that throughout the classical Hollywood period films tended to give us opportunities to identify with heterosexual male heroes and to desire beautiful women. The classical Hollywood film repeatedly coordinated the three gazes we just mentioned (the camera's, the male protagonist's, and the audience's) to position us with the male hero looking at the objectified female. This system (in coordination with society's early twentieth-century attitudes about women) helped give female characters a passive sense of "to-be-looked-at-ness." These glamorous women functioned as a visual spectacle that encouraged male characters (and the film audience that identified with these protagonists) to desire them sexually.

Because we have been placed in this pleasurable position repeatedly over time, these identifications have left their mark on our visual storytelling language. The camera positions and movements are not gender neutral, according to Mulvey. You cannot isolate the cinematic technology and language from its history, because that history shaped what various shots *mean* within that language. Throughout the classical Hollywood period, audiences were asked to adopt a heterosexual masculine position as we looked at shots that began at beautiful women's ankles and proceeded up their glamorously clothed bodies to their perfectly lit faces. This history affects how audiences interpret that simple shot. We know that this shot feminizes and objectifies; that is what this shot *means*.

"OK, maybe this was true a long time ago, but our society has changed," you might argue. "We don't think of women in the same way anymore. And we have female directors nowadays. Doesn't that make the portrayal of women better?" Certainly our images have changed over the years, and clearly we have had many women mediamakers (from Agnes Varda of *The Gleaners and I* to Shonda Rhimes of *Grey's Anatomy*), but Mulvey points out that improving women's images is more complicated than simply putting more women behind the camera (though that is certainly a fine goal). Male and female mediamakers both have to use the cinematic language that they have inherited. No one can reinvent the language by him/herself; it takes years of effort to change such a long-term pattern in language. Mulvey emphasizes that the history of character identification in Hollywood has created a cinematic "language" that constrains what male and female mediamakers can "say." Just as no one can communicate outside of language, no female mediamaker can step outside the gendered history of how shots make meaning.

"But modern movies don't just show men ogling women. They show us women 'checking out' men, too. Directors aren't limited like they used to be in the old days." Of course you're right; female characters do look at men onscreen much more than in the classical Hollywood era. Yet even today there is still something feminizing about the visual system that Mulvey described. Yes, we can put a man into the shot we have been discussing, starting at his ankles and slowly slipping up his body. Such a shot, however, tends to feminize that man. Whenever a man is put on display as the passive object of a lustful gaze in media, that gaze usually "softens" the man. Think of Brad Pitt in *A River Runs Through It*; Leonardo DiCaprio in *Titanic*; Patrick Dempsey ("McDreamy") in *Grey's Anatomy*; any male fashion model; or any male pinup idol from James Dean to the Jonas Brothers. Placing any body (male or female) in the position of passive visual spectacle seems to duplicate the feminizing dynamic developed in classical Hollywood identifications.

If media offer the spectacle of a male body for us, that body had better be doing something active. Physical activity gives heterosexual men a socially acceptable reason to look at another man's body without fear of being accused of homosexual desires. After all, they're marveling at the form of Kobe Bryant's jump shot or enjoying the manly battles in *300*. They're not "checking out" Kobe or the Spartans. Physical activity helps disguise and deflect the sexual voyeurism involved in the gaze. But place the same hypermasculine bodies of NBA (National Basketball Association) players or the half-clothed torsos of gladiators in a passive pinup pose (lying back on one elbow, perhaps), and they are instantly feminized. Placing male bodies as passive objects-of-the-gaze can also dependably produce comedy, as Ben Stiller demonstrates in *Zoolander*.

Although modern media may offer different "hunks" for our visual pleasure than the classical Hollywood cinema did, the visual language that structures our gaze may not have changed dramatically.

"What about the latest generation of kick-butt women in media? Don't they change our images of women?" Certainly women from Sarah Connor in *Terminator 2* to Sarah Michelle Gellar in *Buffy the Vampire Slayer* seem a far cry from the passive visual spectacles of the classical Hollywood pinup girl. And yet notice how conventionally attractive these action heroines are, ensuring that audiences do not have to sacrifice the pleasures of "to-be-looked-at-ness" when watching these powerful women.

My goal here is to start the discussion about the interaction among attractiveness, activity, passivity, the gaze, masculinity, femininity, and identification in modern media, not to provide a definitive explanation. Does Mulvey's theory still have influence in contemporary media? Has the gendered history of spectator positioning fundamentally altered the basic visual language of the camera? How does our previous history of character identification shape our current relations with film and television characters?

What are the components of identification?

In the previous section we introduced the idea of how film and television combine visual and narrative techniques to encourage us to identify with characters. Now let's look more closely at how such strategies interact. Murray Smith has argued that "identification" is too large a term, that it refers to too many different things. He suggests that we break "character engagement" into smaller processes that we can examine more closely. Theories of spectator positioning help us understand how identification can be so powerful when we are immersed in a film. Smith's system helps us explain more precisely how our engagement varies from character to character.

Whenever we gain information about a character, Smith calls this *alignment*. In Smith's terms, we are "aligned" with anyone who appears onscreen. When a wounded person is wheeled into the emergency room in *ER*, we can potentially identify with any person we see (the patient, doctors, nurses, emergency medical technicians, family members) because we have at least some information about who these people are. Even when characters do not speak or move, we get information simply by observing their faces, their clothes, their body posture. Every time we see a character onscreen, we learn something about them, even if the character is a bit player. Alignment (the process of giving us access to character information) is necessary before we can engage emotionally with any character. Whenever a new character appears, the film/television program is (in a sense) nominating him/her as someone we might find engaging.

Although we can identify with anyone we see onscreen, films and television programs make it more likely that we will identify with some characters more than others. Mediamakers do this by controlling the information we have about various characters. The difference between a protagonist and a supporting player is that we know more about the protagonist. In Smith's terms, we are more aligned with the main characters. Alignment, therefore, means giving us access to a character's externally observable actions and his/her internal states (thoughts, feelings, memories, dreams).

Media coordinate this access in several ways. Film and television programs follow certain characters more than others, and the more we follow a particular character, the more information we learn about him/her. We see how characters react to new situations, we hear their discussions, and we go where they go. The camera appears to be more spatially attached to the major characters. It stays nearer to them in scenes, giving us more closeups of their faces, spending more time presenting them onscreen. *Spatial attachment* is one way that film and television create stronger alignment with some characters. By following certain characters more than others, by positioning the camera near them, by spending more time with them, the mediamakers tell us which characters they think are more important.

Spatial attachment gives us the kind of information we might get if we were standing close to a character. This information is external: we see what the character is doing, we hear what they are saying. Another way to align us more fully with characters is to have us experience what is going on inside their heads, to give us access to information that we could not see/hear if we were standing nearby. Film and television have developed a range of techniques to show us a character's mental state directly: dream sequences, flashbacks, voiceover, fantasy sequences, and so on. Mediamakers choose to show us some characters' flashbacks and fantasies but not others'. *Grey's Anatomy* follows a large cast of characters, but the initial and final voiceovers are (almost) always Meredith Grey's, allowing us deeper access to the title character's head. We can identify with any of the characters on *Scrubs*, but the series more closely aligns us with J.D., partly because we see many more of his fantasies than any other character's. By providing direct *subjective access* to dreams and memories, we learn about the characters in a different way than if they had simply told us about their dreams and memories aloud.

Point-of-view provides another means of aligning us with a character. Seeing things literally through a character's eyes gives us direct information about how they are perceiving the world. Hearing things from a specific character's perspective also gives us important access to the character. Part of the power of a first-person-shooter game lies in its strong sense of perceptual point-of-view. We rarely glimpse the character who is blasting his/her way through the gameworld, but all our visual and audio perception is filtered through that singular perspective. Everything we know comes through that first-person viewpoint, which powerfully organizes our experience.

Alignment with a character, therefore, depends on spatial attachment (who we follow, who we are near), subjective access (directly showing us internal states), and perceptual point-of-view (both visual and aural). By controlling these three variables, mediamakers align us more strongly with certain characters than others. By giving us longer, closer, more detailed, and more vivid access to these characters, they encourage us to identify with them.

Let us return to the *ER* emergency room. The television show usually coordinates visual and storytelling information to make us more aligned with the doctors. We may follow the doctor into the ER and then see extended closeups of the doctor's face as she struggles to save the patient's life. We may see brief flashes of memory as the doctor remembers a previous patient who died. The camera may present point-of-view shots as the doctor cuts the patient open and desperately watches the monitor. All these techniques align us with the physician.

Or this particular episode might choose to privilege the patient's perspective. A jerky handheld camera might show us the patient's point-of-view of the ceiling lights as she is wheeled into the ER, and the sounds might be garbled as they are filtered through the injured person's perception. The camera might follow the patient as various medical personnel examine her, giving the confused person multiple closeups. We might even glimpse a drug-addled fantasy from inside the patient's mind.

Alignment (in Smith's terms) is something that the mediamaker chooses. We don't have a choice about which characters the story follows in a film or television program. If you are more interested in the witch than Dorothy in *The Wizard of Oz*, you still have to be aligned with the young girl if you are watching the film at all. (For alignment with the witch, you may have to watch the musical *Wicked*.) Alignment with a character depends solely on the information we are given by the film. It does not commit you to identify with the protagonist, though alignment tends to make it easier for us to identify.

When we receive information about characters, we are often expected to go further than simply understanding them. Mediamakers also encourage us to make moral judgments about the characters, and this also is a crucial component of our character engagement. Smith calls the moral evaluation of a character "*allegiance.*" Often a mediamaker shows us a character's actions so that we can see their moral stance toward the world. By emphasizing how hard the detectives and lawyers work to achieve justice on *Law and Order*, the show encourages us to see them as admirable. The early portions of *The 40-Year-Old Virgin* are designed so that we will evaluate Andy Stitzer as a nice, well-intentioned, sweet, likable guy. If we make these judgments, we are more likely to care about what happens to these characters. Allegiance calls upon our broadly held social principles (we tend to value hard work and niceness) to encourage a dependable audience reaction to the characters.

Just as film and television have created many techniques to promote alignment, the media have also found reliable ways to gain our allegiance. They can show a character committing an act of kindness and generosity. If they show a chase scene, we tend to favor the character being pursued, even if we don't know anything else about either character. In addition, we tend to evaluate characters positively if they are good at what they do. This tendency can encourage us to become allied with some fairly unsavory characters. For instance, Dr. Gregory House may be an insensitive louse on *House*, but we excuse him partly because of his brilliance. Simon Cowell may be personally abusive and smug on *American Idol*, but he is undeniably successful. Hannibal Lecter in *The Silence of the Lambs* is an unrepentant serial killer, but part of his charm is that he is so expert at what he does.

Although character actions are important clues for our moral evaluation, there are other ways to signal how we should judge a character. Casting can play a role in our evaluation because we remember an actor's previous roles when we spot them in a new role. Because we have seen John Cusack play a range of likable characters (from *Say Anything* to *2012*), a mediamaker can assume that we will assign a certain amount of goodwill to the next character he plays. Even if the actor is unfamiliar, his/her "look" can tell us how to "read" the character, and stylistic techniques (such as music, lighting, and camera angle) can accentuate this effect. For instance, when we see Toht the Nazi for the first time in *Raiders of the Lost Ark*, we are supposed to label him as evil (even before he does anything). A jarring musical chord punctuates the low angle closeup as we see his beady eyes and his thin lips. The language of media clearly tells us, "This is the bad guy." Once we decide who the morally preferable characters are, this encourages us to identify with them.

Notice that I used the words "morally *preferable*." Any film or television program is a closed system that presents a limited range of characters. One way to encourage us to identify with an immoral character is to surround that person with even more evil characters. Our only choices are to identify with the least morally objectionable person or to reject identification with anyone. In *GoodFellas* we are more likely to identify with mobster Henry Hill (Ray Liotta) because our other choices are more reprehensible. Henry seems relatively moral compared to sadists like Tommy DeVito (Joe Pesci). Reality television producers can cast their shows to create a network of scheming characters, which encourages us to evaluate which is the least obnoxious of the participants. Allegiance with a character does not mean that we approve of everything they do. It simply means that they are morally preferable to our other options for identification.

Now that we have the more specific concepts of alignment and allegiance, we can describe more precisely how film and television programs encourage our identification with particular characters. In most media, alignment and allegiance work together to help us identify with the protagonists. We follow the main characters as they do likable actions, seeing point-of-view shots from their perspectives, closeups of their reactions, and flashbacks of their memories. This places us in a good position to identify with Andy Stitzer in *The 40-Year-Old Virgin* or Chandler Bing in *Friends*.

In other media, alignment and allegiance interact in complicated ways. When watching *A Clockwork Orange*, we have little choice but to be aligned with Alex, the gleeful, brutal sadist. Since the film follows him wherever he goes (even when he rapes women and beats the elderly), we must either follow him as well or abandon the film. We are, of course, expected to judge his actions harshly, and so our allegiance complicates our engagement with him. Similarly, we have complex engagement with the boss on *The Office* (either the American supervisor Michael Scott or the British David Brent). We spend a considerable amount of time with him, but his pompous attitude and his overbearing actions lead us to see him as a jerk. To say that we simply identify with Alex, Michael, or David does not capture the way these specific media blend moral and visual perspectives. Alignment and allegiance help us explain the complicated mix of pleasures these texts present.

Alignment and allegiance help us understand what was "new" about the stalker films of the 1970s and 1980s, and why these seemed like a disturbing social trend. There was nothing new about seeing beautiful, scantily clad women attacked with a knife. However, when director John Carpenter placed the camera behind Michael Myers's mask in

Halloween, American audiences had the unsettling, protracted experience of stalking the victim through the killer's eyes. Yes, this encourages us to identify with a mad killer, but our new critical language helps us explain this phenomenon more carefully. *Halloween* forces us to be aligned with Michael Myers, while at the same time it expects us to be morally repulsed by the brutal slayings.

In our alignment, *Halloween* emphasizes the visual point-of-view shot over other techniques (we get no flashbacks from Michael and our early glimpses of him are brief). Though one might assume that the perceptual point-of-view shot is the most powerful way to align us with a character, *Halloween* shows us that point-of-view can actually hide character information. In the opening sequence of the film, we see the stalker's visual perspective through the mask, but we know little else about the killer. We get much more information about the victim: we hear her protests, we see her frightened face. We are therefore aligned with both victim and killer in different ways: we get Michael's visual and auditory perspective, while we see and hear the woman's emotional reactions. Because we are denied access to Michael's face, the film is able to conceal a crucial fact about the character: that the killer in the initial scene is a young boy. In this instance, the point-of-view shot (which usually reveals character) actually hides information about the character. Each individual film and television program promotes our identification with some characters, discourages us from identifying with others, and complicates our engagement with still others. Alignment and allegiance give us a language for discussing how this process works.

The limits of identification

Notice that we are beginning to discuss identification with multiple characters, not just a single protagonist. Although a film or television program may cause us to be more aligned with the main character, this does not mean that we can only identify with the protagonist. Linda Williams has argued that although the process of spectator positioning emphasizes one character's perspective over another's, the actual process of real people identifying with characters is more fluid. In all likelihood, we identify with both members of a romantic/sexual couple (according to Williams) and both pursuer and pursued in a chase. We identify in different ways with each, however. Identification for Williams is *multiple simultaneous identification*.

Also notice that we are distinguishing between actual people's identification and "spectator positioning." Remember that the "spectator" is a position; it's not a person. Every film creates a theoretical position that you can occupy to receive maximum pleasure. If everything is working perfectly and you are totally immersed in the film, you (the actual person) are occupying the spectator position. Most media experiences, however, fall short of this ideal. Sometimes you the actual audience member occupy the spectator position and gain pleasure from the film. At other times when the film is not quite "working" for you, you are outside the spectator position. Even when you are not fully caught up in a film, you can still recognize what the film is asking you to feel and think. You can still recognize the spectator position even if you yourself are not occupying it.

Throughout this chapter I have been assuming that films and television programs are trying to get you to identify with characters. Although most mainstream media do this, some mediamakers (particularly those influenced by Bertolt Brecht) intentionally aim to keep us at a distance, to discourage us from putting ourselves in the protagonist's place. By distancing ourselves from a character, we can potentially judge their actions in a more even-handed, less biased fashion. Some have said, for instance, that certain melodramas (such as those made by Douglas Sirk in the 1950s, including *Written on the Wind* and *Imitation of Life*) veer so wildly from one implausible plot turn to another that it is impossible to identify with their female characters in a realistic fashion. Such melodramas serve less as a tear-jerker and more as a social critique of the impossible position of women in the 1950s.

> *Bertolt Brecht* (1898–1956) was an influential German playwright who believed that typical realistic theater encouraged audiences to enjoy themselves for an evening without relating the play to their everyday lives. His plays were full of interruptions and other devices that kept audiences from getting swept up in the story. By startling the audience out of their complacency and distancing them from the characters, Brecht hoped that his theater would have a stronger political effect. His plays include *The Threepenny Opera, Mother Courage and Her Children*, and *The Caucasian Chalk Circle.*

Not all mediamakers want their audiences to be caught up in a realistic story and to identify with the characters, because those emotional experiences can blur the audience's judgment. Lars von Trier's *Dogville* is staged on a skeletal, theatrical-looking set without doors or walls, which helps keep the audience from getting immersed in a realistic space. Dennis Potter's *The Singing Detective* interrupts its hospital scenes with elaborate musical productions in which patients and doctors lip-synch old pop songs. These mediamakers intend for their audiences to be "kicked out" of their normal habits of identifying with characters and immersing themselves in a story. Such mediamakers believe that identification tends to bring us too close to characters, providing a cheap emotional pleasure instead of a useful critical distance. Not every mediamaker has identification as a goal.

Regardless of their intention, no mediamaker can completely control your identifications with characters. No mainstream mediamaker can force you to identify with a character, nor can any art cinema director entirely prevent you from engaging emotionally with a character. We have been discussing two processes (alignment and allegiance) that are components of identification, and these processes can work together to encourage you to identify, but these processes stop short of actual character identification. We can understand characters and morally evaluate them without ever committing our feelings to them.

Films and television programs can provide powerful invitations for us to identify with characters, but they can do no more than invite. You the individual can choose to accept or reject the invitation created by the media. There are many reasons that an individual might reject the spectator positioning. You may encounter a moment that feels "false" (or "unrealistic" or "implausible"; see Chapter 2), and that may kick you out of the story. You may be unconvinced by an acting performance, or the plot might confuse you. Sometimes you may reject the spectator position because your own values differ from the broadly held social values that allegiance uses. For instance, you probably recognize that *The 40-Year-Old Virgin* wants you to find its protagonist Andy Stitzer to be likable and his friends to be horny losers. You, on the other hand, may find his slacker friends to be a welcome relief from Andy's uptightness, and so you may identify more closely with them than with the protagonist. You recognize how you're "supposed" to evaluate Andy as morally preferable by broadly held social standards, but you the individual may substitute an alternate set of values. The film more strongly aligns us with Andy than with his friends, but you may choose to give your feelings to his buddies instead. Since alignment gives us information on several different characters, and media offer us multiple simultaneous identifications, you may identify with characters that the film/television program does not highlight.

Sometimes you can refuse the spectator position for reasons that have little to do with the specific film or television program. If you dislike action films or chick flicks or sitcoms, it may be impossible for these media to entice you into the spectator position. Or your refusal may be more idiosyncratic. I, for instance, have an irrational dislike of

Meg Ryan. I understand that in most of her films I'm supposed to find her cute and adorable. I don't. I recognize the spectator position that a Meg Ryan film creates, but I stubbornly refuse to occupy it. For some pig-headed reason, I deny myself the pleasure of identifying with any character that Meg Ryan portrays, and so I refuse the pleasure that a Meg Ryan film offers. That is my privilege as a moviegoer with free will. I, Greg M. Smith, am not the spectator, and neither are you. The spectator is a temporary position created by the film, a position that promises you and me the pleasure of identification.

This chapter has focused on the power of identification and how film and television have developed many techniques for encouraging that experience, but I end this chapter by acknowledging the limits of identification. Films create spectator positions for us to occupy, but whether any particular individual occupies those positions is not predictable. Identification can be widely shared among members of an audience, but it is also individual. Therefore I end this chapter with a caution about writing about film and television. When you discuss a media text (particularly one you love), it is tempting to say that film/TV *makes* people feel a particular way. After all, that's how it feels. When other people in a movie theater laugh or cry when you do, it's easy to assume they're feeling the same way you do. I urge you to remember that we are all individuals making our own sense out of the images we see. You have no direct way of knowing how other people feel about a film or television program unless you ask them. It is tempting to assume that because you feel something when watching, other people must feel the same, but remember that anyone can reject a film or television program's call to identify with characters. Because identification is remarkably complex, you cannot assume someone is identifying with a character. What you *can* do is describe how the film/television program makes its appeal, how it uses various techniques to encourage us to identify, and how it offers pleasure as a reward. Identification is powerful, but it is not all-powerful.

Bibliography

Metz, C. (1977) *The Imaginary Signifier: Psychoanalysis and the Cinema*, C. Britton, A. Williams, B. Brewster, and A. Guzzetti (trans.), Bloomington: Indiana University Press.

Mulvey, L. (1975) "Visual Pleasure and Narrative Cinema," *Screen* 16.3: 6–18.

Smith, M. (1995) *Engaging Characters: Fiction, Emotion, and the Cinema*, Oxford: Oxford University Press.

Williams, L. (1989) *Hard Core: Power, Pleasure, and the "Frenzy of the Visible,"* Berkeley: University of California Press.

Chapter 4

Genre shmenre

You use the concept of "genre" whenever you are not quite sure what film or television program to watch. If you are not planning to see a particular show ("This series is supposed to be really good") or the work of a specific director or star or national industry ("Let's go see the new Quentin Tarantino film," or "I love French films"), any discussion about media choice probably involves genre:

"What are you in the mood to see?"
"How about a romantic comedy?"
"Nah, we just saw one last week. How about a thriller?"
"I'm not looking for anything that will make me too keyed up. It's been a tough day."

Conversations like this one implicitly acknowledge the way that genre allows us to predict and manage our viewing experiences. Although you haven't seen the latest romantic comedy, you can reasonably expect it to present similar emotional payoffs to ones you have previously seen. You can use genre to manage your mood; if most thrillers make you tense (or amuse or disgust you), you can predict how choosing to see a new thriller might affect your attitude on a given day.

Such decisionmaking recognizes the central consumer difficulty of going to a movie theater or renting a DVD of a TV series: You pay your money before you know if you will like the product, and so you use a shortcut method to predict which films and television programs you will enjoy so that your money will hopefully not be wasted. Therefore, the film and television industry faces a difficult challenge (as do many of the "culture industries"). Film and television are mass production businesses; they produce and distribute their product worldwide to generate large profits. Like any big industry, they try to standardize their business to maximize efficiency. The product they create, however, is not standard. Every film and every television episode is different, unlike (for instance) every can of mass manufactured soup. The reason that you buy a particular brand of soup at the grocery is that the brand guarantees a consistency of taste. One can of soup should dependably taste like any other can of the same brand. Unlike canned soup, every film and every television episode is unique, but media consumers similarly rely on a "brand." With very few exceptions (Disney, Pixar), the "brand" is not the company (not many people say, "Let's go see a Dreamworks picture!"). In film and television, the "brands" are stars (both actors and directors) and genres. Consumers cruising the aisles of a video store (or putting titles in their online media queue) will use stars and genres to guide their purchasing choices. You might say, "I've liked Tina Fey in other things, so I'll probably like her next project." The logic here is somewhat faulty and can lead consumers into choices that don't pay off. You trust the star to be discriminating enough to choose a good project, but of course the star is only one element contributing to the whole.

A film or television program's genre does not guarantee that you will like the product, but genre can help you match the program's overall tone with your current preference. When you feel like watching a sitcom, you can use that category to help you find an appropriate viewing choice. But what is a genre, exactly? Is it more than an aid for choosing videos? And what difference does a genre make today, when film and television seem to put mix genres like cocktails in a blender? In an era when we have Western/science fiction combinations (*Firefly*) and horror comedies (*Scary Movie*), what functions do genres serve?

The components of a genre

"Genre" is simply the French word for "type" or "kind"; the word itself means nothing more elaborate than that (if you want something to sound more sophisticated, say it in French. Film studies academics like to talk about directors as "auteurs" because it sounds classier than "authors"). Not all categories of films/TV programs are referred to as a "genre," however. We can group together all the media made within a country's borders and call it "Japanese film" or "British television," but that is usually considered to be a "national cinema" or "national media industry." The output of an entire country's industry (from drama to comedy to avant-garde works) is usually too varied to have the consistency that we typically expect from a genre. Everything made by a particular studio (Universal, Warner Bros.) or shown on a broadcast television network (CBS, BBC) does not group together into a genre unless that network/studio is designed around a specific genre (the Sci-Fi network, for example). When we group together all the works by a single director/producer (John Ford, Dick Wolf) or actor (Alec Baldwin, Meg Ryan), this rarely produces a genre, though there may be considerable overlap between a mediamaker's work and a preferred genre (John Ford tended to make Westerns, but not exclusively; Dick Wolf is usually associated with TV police procedurals). Not every type or kind of film and television program, therefore, creates a genre. Not every way of classifying media produces the consistency expected in a classical genre.

A classical genre gives both mediamakers and audiences a set of *internally consistent expectations to share*. These expectations serve as a kind of "*code*" that mediamakers use when they create film/television and that viewers use when they watch. Secret codes are useful to real-life spies because they convey meaning to a select group of people. A coded meaning can only be understood by those who know the code key, the set of rules for reading this particular language. Media genre "codes" are usually not so secretive, but they do provide guidelines for how you should interpret story events. When events are placed within the context of a genre, they mean something different than they do in real life; they are coded and interpreted according to different rules. When a friend tells us that they had an exciting day in the real world, we usually ask them to tell us the details, and they begin retelling their day. When someone in a musical says, "Tell us what happened!" this is a sure sign that a musical number will follow (an unlikely occurrence in everyday life).

To mediamakers and audiences who know the codes of the genre, this provides a common "language" that makes genre storytelling efficient and pleasurable. Media-savvy audiences know how common situations in a genre usually unfold. We know that characters in a sitcom tend to learn moral lessons when they resolve their plotlines, and so part of the sitcom's pleasure is seeing exactly how this particular episode will arrive at the moral. This repeatable familiarity is part of what we want when we choose a genre. But we generally do not want to see exactly the same narrative situation over and over, and so we seek out variations in familiar genre elements. *Seinfeld* is undeniably a sitcom, but yet its characters never learn moral lessons; they remain unrepentantly persnickety. By varying this expectation within the sitcom genre, the makers of *Seinfeld* provide a different pleasure, a twist on what we have come to anticipate. Acknowledging these codes can provide fodder for parody, as when Monty Python lampoons the musical convention mentioned above. In *Monty Python and the Holy Grail*, Prince Herbert of Swamp Castle tends to burst into song when given the opportunity to tell a story, and his father (an obvious musical hater) interrupts, waving off the rising strings before the musical number can begin. This joke is made possible because we are aware of the conventional code of musicals.

Genre codes provide mediamakers with the opportunity to confirm or tweak our expectations, and both choices give different pleasures. Reusing codes helps satisfy our desire for a predictably repeatable experience, while varying the genre elements gives us the pleasure of surprise. Genre mediamakers therefore balance predictability and variation throughout a film or television program. A genre, therefore, is more than just a useful *guide to media consumer purchases*. It also *shapes our narrative expectations* from moment to moment.

You may think of genre mediamaking as less creative because it relies on conventional formulas, but consider another way to look at genre storytelling. Rather than holding creativity back, genre codes make certain kinds of storytelling possible. The rigid format of the sonnet did not restrict William Shakespeare's or Elizabeth Barrett Browning's poetic expression; instead, the sonnet gave form to their voices. Genre mediamaking is not less creative because it uses storytelling formulas. Genre provides narrative building blocks that mediamakers can combine in innovative ways. In fact, the way we often recognize innovation is by spotting how this particular mediamaker does things differently from the expected norm. Genre codes set the standard of expectations that makes it possible to see creative variations more clearly. It is no coincidence that many of our greatest mediamakers have worked within established genres. We can easily recognize the achievements of an Alfred Hitchcock or a David Chase when we look at how they rework elements provided by genres (the thriller, the gangster narrative) into distinctive works (*North by Northwest*, *The Sopranos*).

No mediamaker starts from scratch; everyone borrows techniques from their predecessors. "Creativity" and "convention" are not polar opposites. Convention makes a certain kind of creativity possible. Playing with genre elements and reconfiguring them into new arrangements requires a particular kind of imagination. There is fine work and crappy work done in genre mediamaking, just as there is inspired and uninspired work done outside of genre and its codes.

What are these "genre codes?" First of all, they are more specific than the building blocks of film and television in general. We know that we are near the beginning of a television program when we see the opening credit sequence and near the end when we see the closing credit roll. We expect that a film will introduce us to all its main characters within the first half hour. We anticipate that stories in both film and television will move forward in time unless they explicitly signal that a flashback is occurring. These are important overall codes of film and television storytelling, but they do not distinguish one type of program from another. These are part of the "language" of visual storytelling developed by previous mediamakers. Genre codes, however, help us distinguish one type of program/film from another.

We can think of these codes as recognizable *components* of a genre, as elements that can be mixed and matched to make a new film or television program. Genres tend to favor certain kinds of *characters* that serve dependable story functions. Neighbors are useful in sitcoms because they can drop by frequently (without the time-consuming process of knocking) to cause trouble or to listen to other characters. Investigative teams on police procedurals often use characters who can dependably voice certain positions: the brilliant lab technician (who is often socially inept); the weary veteran investigator; the by-the-book administrator; the irreverent bad boy/girl who wants to bypass the legal system; and so on. Westerns need both schoolmarms and barmaids to create two different snares for the roving cowboy. The gunfighter is tempted by the charms of civilization (represented by the "nice girl" schoolmarm) or of sexuality (the barmaid is Western code for "prostitute"), both of which threaten to keep him from riding off into the sunset. Genre films and television programs can reconfigure characters to stage an infinite number of conflicts.

Genres are often recognizable by certain *common images*: tumbleweeds and guns for the Western, the top hat and cane of the musical, large tags with contestants' first names in game shows, uniform jerseys in sports broadcasts, the spaceships of science fiction, and so on. Genre media combine images and characters into standard *narrative situations*: science fiction's climactic battles between space armadas; sports media's replaying of athletic highlights; the love triangle in soap opera; and the "meet cute" of the romantic comedy (an awkward first encounter between soon-to-be-lovers). Genres are not simply collections of concrete elements such as objects and characters. They also consist of the relationships among those elements, arranged into common story patterns and situations.

Places/spaces can also provide recognizable markers of a genre: the interrogation room of the police procedural; the office for the workplace sitcom; the living room sofa that is the centerpiece of classic sitcom action; the newsroom where news is broadcast; the desk and chair set of the talk show; the Western's barroom and open prairies; and the film noir's rain-soaked nighttime urban streets. *Time* is also part of the setting. For instance, not every film set in the American West is a Western (*Chinatown* and *Leaving Las Vegas* take place west of the Mississippi

River, but neither is a Western). Westerns occur in a particular period of time (after the Civil War but before 1900), just as film noir tends to take place in the 1940s and 1950s. The "look" of a genre often depends on creating a world that evokes a particular time and place, down to the characters' costumes and hairstyles, the correct iconographic images, and evocative locations.

Stylistic patterns also can help us identify a genre, though style alone rarely defines a genre. Genres do have stylistic hallmarks: the light through Venetian blinds and world-weary voiceover in film noir; the game show's bright flashing lights; the splashy graphic transitions of sports broadcasts; the headline crawl at the bottom of the news screen; and the classic sitcom's laugh track. Genres also gravitate toward certain key *themes*, such as the Western's negotiation between wilderness and civilization or the game show's competition that balances luck and skill. The musical often stages a conflict between different notions of work and play, while science fiction narratives pose questions about the trade-offs between technology and humanity. Sitcom plots often revolve around the actions of a central troublemaker who must learn how to act more like the more "mature" characters, and so the sitcom shows the tension between "normalcy" and "eccentricity." Though themes are important to genres, they rarely define them, with the possible exception of the social problem film (from *I Am a Fugitive from a Chain Gang* to *Erin Brockovich*), which focuses on a single theme: the battle between an individual and a social institution (from the prison system to big business).

A robust thematic tension helps sustain the vitality of a genre over time. Our society will probably never decide how much wildness we desire versus how much civilization. We recognize the need both for institutions and for crusaders to change them. Each one of us needs to find the balance between work and play, between normalcy and difference. There is no definitive resolution for these tensions, and so genre films and television programs can explore these tradeoffs many times without repeating themselves.

Theme, style, setting (time and place), narrative situation, imagery/iconography, and character: these can all be considered characteristics of a genre. Describing a film or television program in this way makes genre sound fairly static, like preparing a recipe: Choose an element from column A, one from column B, and mix together. A living genre, however, changes over time; the rulebook/cookbook is more dynamic. Rick Altman emphasizes the distinction between the more stable building blocks of genre (things like character type, imagery, and setting) and the relationships between those elements (the connections provided by narrative situations and theme).[1] In certain periods of a genre's development, genres act more like a set of elements that can be combined according to well-understood principles. Genre mediamaking needs this consistency, but such repetition eventually becomes tiring (and less profitable), encouraging mediamakers to explore variations in how those elements are configured. Changing the relationships among the elements changes the genre, creating a new set of genre principles for how to combine elements. Then a genre can use those new principles in stable, recognizable ways.

For example, the Western operated through the 1930s and 1940s according to a fairly recognizable code, producing numerous films about cowboy outsiders who had to decide whether to assist the townspeople in distress. Once this set of elements became overused, filmmakers began exploring alternative configurations of plot and theme. The 1950s experimented with films where the Western hero took action for far more personal reasons. Some cowboy heroes in the 1950s pursued the bad guys because they wanted vengeance for wrongs done to their loved ones, not because they were acting on behalf of the community. The Western protagonist became darker, drawn into a violent vendetta. This new figure altered the conventional codes of the Western; a new character (the reluctant hero) helped generate new films that function according to these new expectations. At any particular moment, a genre can appear static. Over time, however, a genre changes by swinging back and forth between stable codes and variations. The codebook/cookbook is updated by mediamakers responding to the economic/artistic pressure for variation.

Changing characteristic elements can modify the genre itself, but not all elements are equally important to the genre's definition. Setting (both in time and place) is hugely important in labeling media as "a Western" or as "science fiction" but less crucial in musicals or sitcoms, though there are place associations in all media. Many sitcoms take place in modern domestic living rooms, but so do other genres (the soap opera, the family melodrama). A living room set does not clearly signal "this is a sitcom" in the way that a bright "contestant's row" alerts us immediately that this is a game show. The living room couch suggests that it might be a sitcom, and punchlines and a laugh track might confirm that guess. A dramatic confrontation on the couch about infidelity, on the other hand, might lead us toward labeling this soap opera or melodrama.

---

1 Altman calls the building blocks "semantic" and the relational connections between those elements "syntactic," making a comparison between genre and language. The more stable elements function like the semantics of a language (the words), and the connections between them function like syntax (the grammar rules that determine how words fit together into sentences).

Setting therefore evokes the sitcom genre, but place is not as central to the genre's definition as the saloon and the prairie are to the Western. Narrative patterns more clearly distinguish the classic sitcom (the rhythm of setup and punchline), just as the musical depends on the alternation between performed numbers and more naturalistically acted dialogue scenes. Although all genre elements contribute, genres arrange their characteristic elements into a loose hierarchy that makes certain elements more central.

Genre as a critical tool

We have been discussing genres as a shared set of components that make it possible for mediamakers and audiences to connect. Genre serves as a *blueprint for mediamakers*, guiding them as they recombine elements into new films and television programs. For audiences, genre acts as a label that allows them to recognize how this particular film/ television program is likely to operate. In addition, genres are useful to critics for grouping media together in ways that provide insight. A genre, therefore, can be something articulated by a critic, and this version of a genre may not be exactly the same as a mediamaker blueprint or an *audience label*.[2] A critic does not necessarily group film and television programs to guide future media production or to market film and television programs to audiences. A textual critic can define a genre to show connections that mediamakers and audiences have not yet noticed.

Such critics usually acknowledge that our everyday understandings of a genre are not very precise. Everyone can recognize a musical, but what is a musical exactly? Every film that has music cannot be a musical, since almost every film has a soundtrack. Perhaps every film or television program where song and dance are performed is a musical? But how many musical numbers make the media a "musical?" If the characters wander briefly into a club where a band is playing or if a detective (inevitably) visits a strip club, do these musicians and dancers make the overall text a musical? When the three shark hunters in *Jaws* start singing "Show Me the Way to Go Home," does *Jaws* become a musical? What about biographies of musicians, such as *Ray* or *Walk the Line*? How about a recorded concert? Are *The Last Waltz* and *Hannah Montana/Miley Cyrus: Best of Both Worlds* both "musicals" in the same way that *Oklahoma* and *Singin' in the Rain* are? Like many categories that we use unproblematically in the real world, the notion of the "musical" is not so easy to define clearly.

2 This understanding of genre as blueprint and as label comes from Altman.

Rick Altman argues that it is not particularly useful to say that a musical is any film where a character starts to sing or dance. Instead he asserts that the classical film musical has a deeper narrative structure. Altman states that the musical operates differently than Hollywood's typical emphasis on whether an individual hero will successfully accomplish his/her goal. The musical is about a couple, and the outcome is never in doubt: we know that the lovers will end up together. The musical focuses instead on *how* the lovers will overcome their obvious differences to become a couple. One may be uptight, and the other playful, or the differences may involve class, nationality, dress, or any cultural distinction. In *Grease*, for instance, Sandy is a prim, pastel-wearing romantic who is hopelessly devoted to her man. Danny is a leather-clad greaser who is more concerned with looking cool than with making any commitment. No one doubts that these two unlikely lovers will become a happy couple in the end. The progression of the film is to watch how these two characters adjust their attitudes to meet somewhere in the middle. Danny earns a letter in track, and Sandy becomes a leather queen. Along the way, we discover that the two are not as different as they first seemed. In resolving the cultural differences between the two, we acknowledge the need for both personal connection and broader popularity, for romance and sensuality. Any difference in the lover's styles can create tension, and the musical (for Altman) is a film focused on musical performances that resolve the cultural differences between the couple.

This definition does not fit every film that you might consider to be a musical, but Altman asserts that any definition that was all-inclusive ("a musical is any film that anyone considers to be a musical") would be so broad that it would not tell us anything interesting about the films. Fitting every possible film or television program into a genre is an impossible goal for a critic, according to Altman. Instead the critic should aim for a definition that tells us something insightful about the genre and that covers as much as possible of the genre's everyday meaning.

Critics therefore can have different definitions of a genre, each one with a slightly different emphasis. The best definition is the one that most closely matches our everyday understanding while still providing a cohesive structure for the category. It includes as many as possible of the films/television programs that would usually be found in discussions of the genre, and it excludes as many films/programs as possible that would not normally be considered genre members. In this way, the concept of genre serves as a *tool for critical analysis*.

Using genre as a critical tool is different from using it as a media-maker's blueprint or an audience's label. The payoff for a critic's definition of a genre is in the insight it provides into the structures underneath our broad, commonsense category. If the definition provides a new perspective on the genre, then that itself is a valuable exercise. For example, consider Noël Carroll's discussion of what he calls "art horror" (including horror novels, films, and television programs). The crucial factor that distinguishes horror is the presence of what Carroll calls the "horrifying monster." A monster is a being that we believe cannot exist within the natural, scientific order of things. Monsters are impure mixtures of categories that cannot normally be combined: living and dead (vampires, zombies), human and animal (werewolves), human and demon (possession). The other fictional characters in the film/TV program recognize that the horrific monster is threatening and disgusting, and both reactions are important for Carroll. If the monster is only threatening, then he/she elicits fear; if he/she is impure without threatening the characters, the monster is merely disgusting.

This set of rules allows us to distinguish horror from other related media genres. "Suspense" can proceed much like horror (full of chases and danger), but it lacks the supernatural element of the monster. "Science fiction" shows us alien figures that cannot be explained by contemporary science, but the characters do not necessarily respond to these "monsters" with fear and disgust. Chewbacca is a monster (seemingly part animal, part humanoid), but he is not a horrifying one (he hangs out in bars and co-pilots spaceships). A monster may appear in a comedy (such as Frankenstein's appearance in a *Saturday Night Live* sketch with similarly inarticulate Tonto and Tarzan), but the monster's presence alone does not make this "horror," since Tonto and Tarzan do not react with fear or disgust. Horror for Carroll is organized around the threatening, impure, supernatural monster.

Are films/TV programs with serial killers "horror?" Carroll says that depends on the killer. A killer like *Halloween*'s Jason seemingly cannot be harmed by bullets, and so Jason acts supernaturally, even though he is not given an explicitly other-world status. Jason is a horrific monster. Other serial killers (such as *Psycho*'s Norman Bates) are explained in purely psychological terms in ways that make perfect sense, given our current understanding of the human mind. *Psycho* would be better categorized as suspense rather than horror, according to Carroll, though he recognizes how odd it is for a definition of horror to exclude what many would consider a seminal horror film.

Whether or not you agree with Carroll's definition of horror, he provides an instructive example of genre as a critical tool. Carroll chooses one component of the horror film (the disgusting, threatening monster) and places this at the center of his genre hierarchy. He shows how many fictions (films, television shows, novels) that would normally be considered "horror" are covered by his definition, and how this definition usefully separates horror from other genres. He asserts that his definition explains more about horror than any competing explanation (go ahead, try to beat him!), recognizing that no critical understanding of a genre can explain all genre films. Carroll is doing what any textual genre critic does: defining a genre in ways that make the real-world category more consistent and more insightful.

Alternatives to the classical genre

We can now differentiate genre as a critical tool from what Tino Balio calls a *"production trend."* A production trend is how mediamakers label a current film/television category when talking with other media-makers. It is the industry's term for the kinds of texts they are making. Many production trends have the same name as genres. When Hollywood filmmakers created *West Side Story* and *Chicago*, they were aware they were working in the musical genre, and they referred to these films as musicals. When TV production companies created *All in the Family* and *Friends*, they understood that they were making sitcoms. But not every production trend has the internal consistency of a critical genre. For instance, filmmakers may say they are making a "blockbuster film" or an "epic film," but these categories may refer more to film budget or length rather than a cohesive set of components. A "blockbuster" may be action-adventure, fantasy, science fiction, animation, and so on. Similarly, Balio notes that Hollywood studios in the 1930s referred to "prestige pic-tures," a term that referred to big budgets and large promotional efforts. This production trend included biographies, lavish costume adventures, literary adaptations, high profile Westerns, and so on. A category used by mediamakers can be different from the labels used by critics.

Critics can also define genres without relying on mediamakers' terms. The classic example of a "critics' genre" is film noir. Film-makers working on *The Maltese Falcon* in 1941 did not think of them-selves as creating a "film noir"; there was no such category. The term was applied by French critics who saw a whole group of American films made during World War II, which made delayed appearances on French screens after German occupation. When French critics saw America's wartime film output as a group, they spotted a trend that Americans had not noticed: Hollywood films had become darker in tone (and thus the term "film noir," or "black film"). French critics saw a consistency that is the hallmark of a critical genre, even though filmmakers thought of themselves as working within a production trend called the "detective film." The textual genre critic can articulate a pattern in mediamaking without being bound by what the media authors call their work.

You too can create a definition of a critical genre or subgenre: a consistent pattern of media components that helps us group media texts in insightful ways. For example, one might articulate a subgenre of "body switching media," where characters end up inside someone else's body. Such a subgenre would include *All of Me*, *Big*, *Freaky Friday*, *Jack*, the episode of *Buffy the Vampire Slayer* where Faith and Buffy trade bodies, *Vice Versa*, *Switch*, *13 Going On 30*, *Like Father Like Son*, and so on (it's amazing how many of these you can spot, once you start looking for the pattern). Clearly the mediamakers had certain common story patterns in mind when they made these films and television programs, though these tendencies never coalesced into a "production trend" label. These producers did what all mediamakers do: they borrow elements from previous media and rearrange them into new configurations. Textual genre critics can spot consistent patterns in media practice, and they can articulate their own versions of genres and subgenres. Mediamakers and critics have different jobs and can arrive at different groupings. One seeks to create new media; the other tries to discern patterns underneath the mediamakers' practice.

Some production trends that guide mediamakers and audiences act more like an "*address*" than a consistent set of components. Some categories of film and television are based on who is being addressed by the media. For example, what is a "children's film" or "children's television?" How might you describe the defining characteristics of the videos that end up in the children's media category? Some are animated, some are live action. Children's media usually present overt morals, but then so do many mainstream media. Children's media usually feature child protagonists, but there are many films centered on children that would never appear on a children's media shelf (from *The 400 Blows* to *Born into Brothels* and *City of God*). The category of children's media, therefore, is defined more by who these film and television programs address than by any set of components. Children's media have children as an intended audience; they are marketed toward children (or to the parents who pay for their children's viewing); and they have child protagonists. In the classical studio period, Hollywood created a major production trend with a female audience in mind: the "woman's film." Although these films were seen by men, women, and children, they were created with women's tastes in mind (or rather with Hollywood's version of what they thought women liked). These films starred women and were marketed toward women. Like "children's media," the "woman's film" functions more like an address than a set of genre components.

The classical genre not only assumes consistency; it also assumes that the genre continues for a significant period of time. If a cycle of consistent media production occurs over a relatively brief period of time, we usually call this a "*movement*." A movement is a cohesive grouping of media production that is bounded in time (and often also in place). Various New Waves of mediamaking (French, Chinese, Iranian) emerge, but they do not last forever. The Soviet montage cinema, Italian neorealism, and American television anthology drama are all movements; they occurred at a particular place and time. Mediamakers can be inspired by the Soviet montage filmmakers or the Italian neorealists, but they cannot *become* an Italian neorealist or a Soviet montage filmmaker. Those doors opened and are now closed. A genre lasts longer and usually continues to be productive. Although there aren't many new musicals or Westerns any more, mediamakers still can work in both genres.

The *American television anthology drama* was one of the most highly praised programming forms in the so-called "Golden Age" of television in the 1950s. Adapting a program format from radio, the television anthology did not use a continuing set of characters. Instead, it featured a different story with a different cast each week. Anthologies such as *Playhouse 90* and *Studio One* emphasized that these shows were broadcast live (which emphasized their continuity with dramatic theater), and in many cases these broadcasts resemble theater productions staged for television. Later anthology dramas such as *The Twilight Zone* were recorded on film before broadcasting. Memorable productions include *Marty*, *12 Angry Men*, and *Requiem for a Heavyweight*.

Soviet montage filmmaking in the 1920s provided an overtly political alternative to Hollywood's focus on entertainment. While Hollywood used "montage" (editing) to create a sense of continuous time and space, Soviet montage filmmakers saw the technique as a more radical way to shock and energize the viewer. Their editing juxtaposed images in ways that encouraged viewers to become more actively involved in piecing together the story. The stories told by these socialist filmmakers focused on collective heroes rather than the individual hero of the Hollywood film. Although montage cinema was replaced by socialist realism in the Soviet Union in the 1930s, it remained enormously influential on political filmmakers internationally. Key figures include Sergei Eisenstein, Lev Kuleshov, Dziga Vertov, and Vsevolod Pudovkin.

Throughout this chapter we have been classifying whole films and whole television programs. Thomas Schatz has suggested that we might better examine a *"mode"* of expression, a term that can apply to whole films but also to individual scenes. A "mode" makes an appeal to a particular emotion, and modes are often named after those feelings. For Schatz, horror, suspense, and comedy can be modes; they describe the feeling that the film or television program aims to elicit. When an entire film or television program tries to create a horrified, suspenseful, or comic response, these terms are used as genres. In these instances, "genre" and "mode" are the same.

But Schatz proposes that the notion of "mode" can be briefer; it need not apply to a whole film. Media can move into a mode and back out again. A show like *Buffy the Vampire Slayer* switches back and forth between modes: trying to frighten us at times (the horror mode), while at other times making us laugh (the comic mode) or cry (the melodramatic mode). A film like *Speed* lurches back and forth between thriller/suspense and romance. These media do not purely play by one genre's rules. Whole films/TV programs that were squarely within a genre helped set these rules/expectations, but once those rules are established, any individual film or television can evoke those expectations for a scene or two. Genre mediamaking helped create the possibility for film and television to evoke emotion in small doses. This allows mediamakers to use modes of expression in particular scenes instead of being bound to a single genre for an entire film/TV program.

Contemporary mediamakers increasingly combine and blend modes of expression when they make individual films and television programs. Producers today still make pure expressions of genre: straightforward horror films (particularly lucrative in the straight-to-DVD market) and traditional sitcoms (such as *Two and a Half Men*). These whole films and television programs operate within the horizons established by genre. Many other modern media treat genre much as a painter treats colors on a palette, mixing elements to create a distinctive whole. Mainstream blockbuster films combine genre elements to increase their appeal to multiple audiences (the Harry Potter books and films mix fantasy, coming of age narratives, boarding school tales, sports stories, and teen romance). Independent films show off their hipness by refusing to play within classical genre lines, mingling genre components to create odd fictional universes (for example *Donnie Darko*'s mixture of elements from the disaster film, psychotherapy narratives, suburban family melodrama, and the film classic *Harvey*). Many "reality television" programs are hybrids of previous television genres: the soap opera (with its large continuing cast of engaging characters), the game show (with the elimination of characters according to the rules of play), and the documentary (with its emphasis on interviewing).

In classic eras of film and television, mediamakers used genre to provide audiences with the promise of similarity with difference. Any particular piece of genre media reassembled material from previous examples, providing just enough of a twist to lure audiences. Today's mediamakers still rely on genre to provide the right mixture of familiarity and novelty, but many of them feel less constrained to operate solely within a single genre. Instead they take elements from a range of more established genres, sampling more broadly to make their commercial and artistic appeals. Classic and contemporary mediamakers both borrow from previous media, and some current producers take fuller advantage of a media-savvy audience that can shift comfortably from mode to mode and that can recognize elements taken from many genre texts.

Throughout this chapter we have focused on the media texts, on the similarities shared by members of a genre. Some critics have suggested that perhaps we should not emphasize the film and television programs themselves; perhaps we should pay more attention to the way we talk about these programs. Jason Mittell has argued that a genre is more a *cultural concept* than it is a property of film and television programs. For Mittell, a genre is not an internally consistent collection of components that we can spot. Instead, a genre is a cultural category that can describe quite different media. For example, in the classic broadcast television era, Saturday morning was the primary time slot devoted to children's programming, and so we developed a category called the "Saturday morning cartoon." This included cartoons that were originally meant to be seen by diverse audiences as part of an evening's entertainment at the movie theater (such as classic Looney Tunes animation); animation initially developed for prime time television broadcast (such as *The Flintstones*); and limited animation cartoons created specifically to be shown on Saturday mornings (such as *Scooby-Doo*). The production contexts differed greatly for these cartoons, as did their original intended audiences, but still they became recognized as "Saturday morning cartoons." These different media were grouped together by the culture because of certain industrial scheduling practices, not because they were internally consistent.

If we view a genre as a cultural construct, not a property of media themselves, then this may provide insight into categories such as "classic TV" and "reality television." A set of cultural values enshrines *Gilligan's Island* and *The Andy Griffith Show* as "classic," rather than other shows made in the 1960s. Who decides what gets to be included as classic television? And what exactly is "reality television?" What are the consistent components that connect *The Bachelor, The Real World, American Idol, American Chopper, The Osbournes, Project Greenlight, Extreme Makeover, Trading Spaces, Punk'd, Fear Factor, The Deadliest Catch,* and *Wife Swap*? How do you distinguish reality television from the game show or from documentaries with reenactments? We discuss "reality television" as if we all know what that is, but perhaps this category is actually composed of several different kinds of shows. Perhaps this category is primarily a cultural label that we use to group these programs together. You cannot determine a film or television program's genre by simply looking at the text itself, according to Mittell. You need to see how that film or television program is described in the cultural, industrial landscape.

We now have a full range of terms to describe how to group media together, allowing us to have more precise discussions. Is film noir (for example) a genre (in the critical sense or the cultural sense)? Is it a production trend? A mode? An address? A movement? At its beginnings, film noir clearly was not a production trend (a common term used by mediamakers to describe their production), since that term didn't exist. Some could argue that film noir is more of a movement that begins around 1941 and ends near 1958, and that a new genre/production trend called "neo-noir" emerges later (including *Chinatown* and *L.A. Confidential*, films that see themselves as operating according to shared rules of a genre). Thomas Schatz argues that noir is a mode based on anxiety, and that media can shift in and out of this mode (from the "Girl Hunt" gangster-style musical number in *The Band Wagon* to the grim, gritty world of *Blade Runner*).

This little exercise in classification is not meant to arrive at an "is it or isn't it" answer. Instead, I wish to emphasize how our perspective changes as we use one term versus another. If we think of a group of media as a movement, this provides a different emphasis than if we think of the group as an address. The point here is not to determine once and for all how to classify a film or television program. Instead I wish to demonstrate how different classification schemes make us see the media differently. Genre still matters because it structures our expectations for whole films/television shows and for individual moments. Genre still matters because it shapes how we see the media landscape.

Bibliography

Altman, R. (1999) *Film/Genre*, London: BFI Publishing.
Balio, T. (1993) *Grand Design: Hollywood as a Modern Business Enterprise, 1930–1939*, New York: Scribner.

Carroll, N. (1990) *The Philosophy of Horror: Or, Paradoxes of the Heart*, New York: Routledge.

Mittell, J. (2004) *Genre and Television: From Cop Shows to Cartoons in American Culture*, New York: Routledge.

Schatz, T. (1981) *Hollywood Genres: Formulas, Filmmaking, and the Studio System*, New York: McGraw-Hill.

Further reading

Altman, R. (1987) *The American Film Musical*, Bloomington: Indiana University Press.

Part II

Discussing media and society

Chapter 5

"Studies show"

How to understand media violence/effects research

Everybody knows that media cause violence, right? News reports frequently tell us what "studies show," and such quantitative studies often find that violent content in television, movies, and video games is associated with a higher level of aggression in viewers. Because these findings circulate so widely in popular magazines and news programs, many policymakers and parents act as if the link between media violence and real violence were a proven fact.

In your introductory media studies class, you are likely to hear a different depiction of the media. Media studies scholars tend to emphasize the complexity of media and the complicated ways that even ordinary viewers make meanings from them. To think of media as having straightforward "effects" is to do violence to the intricate interaction between films/television/games and their audiences. A media studies class slows down this interactive process, expanding and elaborating on the ways we interpret media every day. Contemporary media scholars (particularly those in the humanities) usually favor ideas about how active audiences engage with media, instead of thinking of how a more passive audience reacts to media.

College students taking required introductory classes in both the social sciences and the humanities can feel like they are being indoctrinated into two different "religions" (Catholicism and Judaism, for instance). You recognize that the two religions are searching for similar things, but they are approaching matters in entirely different ways and they place their faith in very different gods. The word "faith" feels like the right word here because both quantitative and qualitative researchers have core beliefs that are essentially unprovable. Quantitative scholars believe that numbers can provide a usefully clear summary of the world. Qualitative researchers place their faith in the capacity of words to capture the world's nuances. Both approaches have advantages and both have shortcomings.

In an introductory media studies class, you are likely to encounter the many concerns that humanities scholars have about quantitative media research. In general, academics in the humanities believe that numbers are an oversimplification of a complicated world. When you start counting, you tend to emphasize things that are countable and de-emphasize ones that aren't. This means that it is easier to count onscreen punches and tabulate responses on a standardized form than to interrogate the contradictory, sometimes unarticulated meanings that people make out of media.

As a humanities-based scholar, I share this concern. I am aware, however, that this concern is somewhat like a Catholic criticizing Jewish theology. I sincerely believe that my religion has distinct advantages for arriving at the Truth; that's why it's *my* religion. But there is something a bit unfair about criticizing another faith. That's why in this chapter I will stick to criticisms of media violence research that the researchers themselves would agree with. I will articulate concerns from within the paradigm of quantitative research to show that the connection between onscreen violence and offscreen behavior is not as well founded as popular accounts would have you believe.

My academic history helps give me a distinct perspective on quantitative and qualitative media research. I started my undergraduate career pursuing simultaneous interests in computer science and psychology. In my introductory psychology classes I loved reading about what "studies show." When I took upper level methods classes and started reading actual research articles, I was surprised at how much more limited the actual conclusions were than the summaries I had read in my introductory textbooks. As a computer science major, I took math classes alongside the math majors. There I learned about the mathematician's concerns about how social scientists use certain statistical methods. This frustrated psych major and computer scientist later went on to be a humanities scholar who integrates good quantitative research into his own work (on film and emotion).

I do believe that there is such a thing as good quantitative media research. Because of my background, however, I understand just how *hard* it is to do such work. A great many studies on media violence are not particularly well constructed by the strict standards of good quantitative research. Even well-designed and well-implemented studies are frequently exaggerated when their results are summarized in popular press accounts. In fact, the omnipresent understanding that media cause violence can make it more difficult to study to see if this is actually true. I am not a media violence researcher, and I do not envy their job, which seems particularly difficult. I do ask that their research be well constructed and carefully discussed by the standards of their own research paradigm.

If you pin media violence scholars down (pardon the violent act; I've seen too much wrestling on TV), they will tell you a much more humble version of their research findings than the one that circulates in the news. They will say that media have been shown to cause small amounts of aggression in some people for a limited amount of time. This is a far cry from the allegations that media are making our society a more violent place.

This chapter will help you learn how to interrogate media effects studies instead of unproblematically accepting what they "show." Although this chapter focuses on the example of media violence research, the principles I outline here can be applied to any quantitative media effects studies. You won't be an expert in quantitative methods after reading one chapter (this chapter will not enable you to criticize which method of regression analysis a researcher chooses, for instance), but this will give you enough knowledge to make you a savvier consumer of social science research. Most humanities majors only take introductory classes in social science where they read research outcomes, and so most never learn how to critique the research itself. I believe this puts humanities students at a major disadvantage because popular reporting is filled with accounts of what "studies show." Learning to appraise social science research is a basic survival skill in our media-saturated environment.

If you can't be sampled, you can't be studied

If a researcher is studying a fairly small group (for instance, everyone in my immediate family), he/she can actually question each and every person (whether my family of liars and card sharks will answer truthfully is another matter). When studying larger groups, researchers must take a representative sample to stand in for the whole population. The rule is: you can use your sample to make generalizations about everyone who could have possibly been included in that sample. Perhaps more importantly, the opposite is also true: investigators can't generalize about anyone who couldn't possibly have ended up in the sample. The sample defines the population you can discuss. If you can't be sampled, you can't be studied.

The difficulty is that when quantitative researchers summarize their findings, they often leave out the complexities of sampling, thus making it appear that they can explain more than their research can truly justify. Partly this is because of the brevity of summaries, but partly this is because it is not easy to take a sample that could potentially include everyone you want to study in the real world. The trouble occurs when you think you are studying a different group than the one you actually have access to.

Let's say that you want to do a telephone survey. Sounds easy enough, yes? Grab a phone book, randomly sample the entries, and start calling. But remember the principle: if you can't be sampled, you can't be studied. Any limitations in the sampling procedures will change the population you're examining, whether you know it or not. Obviously a telephone survey will only get responses from people who have phones. Given the seeming omnipresence of phones, this may not cause much concern, but this may limit your access to the poorest of respondents. What about unlisted numbers? Does the group of people with listed numbers differ in some way from those without (perhaps introducing a class bias along with a gender factor, with women and upper class people being more inclined to keep numbers private)?

Let's say that you use a computer to generate phone numbers randomly to eliminate this problem. Do you ask questions of the person who answers, even if they're a child, or do you ask for adults only? Even choosing the time to call can have a great bearing on your potential population. Suppose you decide to call between 7:00 and 9:00 p.m. Eastern. This may skew your sample toward the East Coast of the United States, with fewer people in the West at home in this period, or away from people who work the night shift. In addition, conducting your research during the summer may change the population, since more people are on vacation then. Let's say that you do call people at an appropriate hour. What about all the people who hang up as soon as you ask them to do a survey? Do these people differ in some important ways from the ones who do agree to take the time to be surveyed? Do they care more about your topic, or are they lonelier? It's hard to know. But literally the population that you can generalize about is "adults in America who have phones who were at home on June evenings and who were willing to take a survey."

Admittedly, that's a mouthful, and so it's understandable that researchers simply say "Americans." Strictly speaking, however, you can generalize only about this particular group and no one else. To say that you have surveyed "Americans" is overreaching. Good researchers take precautions to limit the difference between the group they are sampling and the group they are describing, but there is always some difference. You may not scrutinize every phone survey this closely, but this simple example shows how you should be skeptical about accepting the summarized generalizations from quantitative research on face value. You should always wonder who is left out of the sample.

Every study takes an imperfect snapshot of the population, and in the detailed writeup of the study every researcher admits the limitations of his/her sampling practices. But one such obviously limited practice has become so commonly used that it has become generally accepted: using students in introductory college classes. You may have been in an intro to psychology class where you were strongly encouraged to participate in a certain number of experiments. This understandably guarantees that professors and graduate students will have a group of available participants for their research. The difficulty lies in how generalizable such studies are.

Again, remember that if someone can't enter into the sample, you can't make generalizations about them. Think about how limited a typical college class is. First of all, college students in general are different from the broader population; they're usually younger, smarter, more affluent. Your particular college has its own distinctive blend of ethnicities, regions, religions, and interests that differs from other institutions. Then consider how those students who sign up for an introductory psych class might differ from those who take an intro to sociology class, or how an 8:00 a.m. class might be different from a 1:00 p.m. class (perhaps the earlier class members were not organized enough to register in time to get a prime class meeting time). Many classes announce a general topic for each experiment, so students can choose an experiment that interests them. Do those students who sign up for a "media" experiment differ from those who sign up for a "childrearing" study?

Each of these factors alters the sample slightly, and each one changes the generalizations possible for the study. It is simply not possible to make claims about "men and women" or even "undergraduates" based on any one study. To be fair, every quantitative researcher understands that any one study only gives a partial glimpse of a phenomenon, and researchers have faith that research (over time) will add glimpse after glimpse until they get a full vista of what is going on. The difficulty is that this humility about the limitations of a single study rarely enters into the article's abstract (the formal summary of the study's outcome), which seems to make bolder claims about what the study shows. It is this larger claim, and not the humbler, more precise one, that gets reported widely.

I understand why academics depend on this available group to continue the massive amount of research done in the social sciences, and I do believe that good work can be done using this group. Studying the college freshman provides a particularly good opportunity for new graduate students to learn research methods, and such research can provide a useful trial to test the study's approach before examining a broader population. But the most studied animal on the planet is the American college freshman, and the question remains: how much can we generalize from this overstudied population?

Never "assume" a random sample

If you take a math class in probability/statistics, every word problem begins in exactly the same way: "Assume a random sample." This is a requirement on which virtually all probability theory is based. If the sample is not random, then the research can only use what are called "descriptive statistics," such as percentages. If 90 percent of the people in a study act a particular way, then that may seem pretty convincing. Researchers, however, understand that percentages can be deceiving. If you choose the right sample, you can arrive at almost any outcome. To prevent any skewing of the sample, quantitative researchers rely on the mathematical notion of random sampling, which enables them to use a different class of statistics ("inferential statistics") that can tell us how dependable the percentage is.

The problem occurs when applying such statistics in the common situation described above: the experiment on the undergraduate class. If you are administering a survey to a class about the kinds of violent programming they watch, there is no way you can assume a random sample, and without that basis you can't make authoritative claims. In one of the most frequent academic research situations, the kinds of claims you can make are limited.

Part of the reason why those math majors in my classes expressed such skepticism about quantitative social science research is because "randomness" is a pure mathematical principle that cannot be taken lightly. The word means something much more specific than its ordinary everyday definition. "Random" doesn't mean "haphazard" or "accidental." The term means that every member of the population has an equal chance of getting into the sample. No one person is more likely to be selected than any other. This requires considerable care on the researcher's part.

Thankfully, researchers have developed ways to dependably generate random numbers (using computers or tables), and they routinely use such methods in their work. For instance, one way to do research effectively using undergraduate classes is to assign the participants randomly into two groups: an experimental group and a control group. Even though the groups were randomly assigned, there would still be limits to how broadly you could generalize, as discussed in the previous section. Careful attention to sampling helps reduce the difference between the population you are truly studying and the one you believe you are studying. Randomness helps ensure that you can confidently generalize from your sample to the larger population.

Random selection makes it possible for researchers to use more powerful statistics. Let's say that you recognize that more women attend your college than men or that the students tend to be more affluent. If you use these students in your media violence study, will you be studying the effects of their habitual viewing habits or will you end up accidentally studying the influence of their gender or socioeconomic level? If most of the people in your sample are upper middle class women, then it is hard to tell what the dominant underlying factor is: their gender, their income, or their viewing habits. Which one is more responsible for your findings? If you randomly select enough participants, you can start dividing the group into smaller groups, and statistics can show you which factors explain more than others: gender, income, viewing habits, or any combination of these.

The key words there are "enough participants." The more times you start dividing your group according to explanatory factors, the more participants you need to make the statistics pay off. Basically the more people you sample, the more accurate a picture of your population you get. This is because of a purely mathematical principle that, unfortunately, has the most easily misunderstood label: "significance."

Not all significant research is "significant"

When you say something is significant, you mean it is important, substantial, meaningful. Unfortunately, statisticians chose to use this same word to describe a very specific mathematical principle, and social science researchers adopted this word, although it causes confusion. When statisticians call research "significant," they mean that it is likely that if you did the research again (choosing another random sample of the same population) you would get the same results. This concept is an acknowledgment that even if you do randomly sample a group it is possible to get a snapshot of the population that is distorted in some way. Maybe you will get all the men in your particular random sample or all the ping-pong players or all the libertarians, and perhaps that will not give you an accurate picture of the overall group. "Significance" (statistically speaking) is a measure of how likely it is that your study randomly chose the wrong people. It is a purely mathematical concept that has little to do with judging how important a research project is.

Imagine, for instance, a study where 40 percent of the people preferred grape slushies and 40.1 percent favored cherry. You might reasonably conclude that this is not a particularly significant difference, in the normal sense of the word. However, in the technical sense of the word, this indeed could be (mathematically) significant if you asked enough people their preference. The study's "significance" is a purely mathematical computation usually performed by computer, and the best way to give your study a good chance of being "significant" in this sense is to include more people. Basically, the more participants you include in your research, the more "significant" the findings are.

Remarkably, it is possible to get a pretty accurate look at the entire United States by randomly sampling a fairly small number of people. If you look at most major polls, you will note that they survey anywhere from 1,000 to 1,800 people, which is not that many people given the size of the entire country. And yet the poll is able to say something like "there's a 95 percent degree of confidence that this poll is within three percentage points." What that means is that if they conducted the poll again with a different random sample, there is a 95 percent chance that the repeated findings would be somewhere between three points lower and three points higher than the original report. So if we repeated our slushie study 100 times, in 95 of those studies the preference for grape would be somewhere between 37 percent and 43 percent. It seems almost magical that statistics can "predict" how repeated studies might turn out, but this confidence is based (for technical reasons) on the magic of random sampling.

So "significance" has a very precise meaning in quantitative research. Of course, this is what academics do: we try to give precise definitions to fuzzy real-world phenomena. In this instance, however, confusion arises from using such a common term to describe a specific technical concept. When researchers describe their work as being "significant," they mean it in the limited mathematical sense. What most ordinary people hear, however, is that the work is "important." Quantitative researchers rarely take the time to educate ordinary people about what "significance" really means, and so the confusion continues. "Significance" means "I've taken the time and effort to study a large enough number of people to be confident that this finding is repeatable," and it means nothing more or less than that. ("Repeatable" may be a better word to describe what researchers mean by "significant.") In fact, as important a figure as Earl Babbie, whose book *The Practice of Social Research* has taught untold numbers of academics how to do basic research, admits a "personal prejudice" against the term. His disagreement is not on statistical grounds but because he is concerned that measures of significance "mislead more than they enlighten" (p. 424). As a student learning to scrutinize studies, you should never assume that because research is labeled "significant" it is also important.

Studies that don't find significant effects are unlikely to be published

Significance in the technical sense is one of the key factors in making research publishable. When researchers crunch the numbers through the computer, they often moan when the computer reports a low significance level in their findings. Usually a study will study several different variables to give a better chance of finding something that is statistically significant. A published study will report if a variable was not shown to have a significant effect, but only if this is included along with other statistically significant findings. A study that gets few or no statistically significant findings will likely not be published.

Doesn't it make sense that academic journals should focus on research that shows an impact? Not necessarily. Finding that a factor has *little* impact can also be an important outcome. Suppose a researcher does a study that finds that media violence has little impact on their population. Given how many people believe that such depicted violence poses a public health risk, this negative finding would seem relatively important. Such a study, however, is relatively unlikely to be published because of journals' preference for statistically significant research. This means that studies that show the effects of media violence are overreported and studies that do not confirm these effects are underreported. We have no way of knowing how many studies have tried to link images of violence to the real world and failed. This publishing preference distorts the overall research picture in favor of the link between media violence and behavior.

It is, of course, in the researcher's own self-interest to emphasize strong findings, not only to academic publishers but to the press when they interview academics. A stronger claim makes a better story, and everyone who has ever given a press interview knows this. I am not accusing media violence researchers of lying or of tweaking their findings in a particular direction. I do wish, however, to point out how many simplifying filters exist between the actual research and its reporting in popular media. First, researchers create an abstract, a summary of the complex research in 50–75 words, as part of every published article. Journalists seek sound bites from academics when they interview them for news stories, and the terser the quotation the better. Quantitative researchers are human, too. Like all academics they have their vanity, and we all want to look good in the public eye. Like all of us, academics are also motivated by money. I recall a conversation with the head of a research center at my university. As I said earlier, I am not a media violence scholar, but I do do work on film and emotion, work that uses quantitative research as a vital source. This center director told me that if I ever considered work on media and violence, the center would be very interested in working with me because "there's always money in media and violence." As the university becomes more dependent on grant money, it is hard for actual human researchers to ignore the financial payoffs of working on the link between media and violence.

Politicians are humans too, and they want to look good in front of their voters, so many have learned that attacking the media is a particularly useful strategy for polishing a political image. It is much easier to deal with the portrayal of criminals in media than it is to solve the ever-present problem of actual crime. Attacking fictional criminals on television, in movies, or in video games, however, *looks* a lot like attacking the real thing. Such a hard-line stance can help counter charges that a political figure is "soft on crime" without ever forcing them to do anything difficult (and costly) to deal with the real-world problem.

I am not suggesting that politicians or quantitative researchers behave unethically. I do think that many political figures believe that media cause violence, and I do believe that media violence researchers work hard to keep their research rigorous. (The smart student should also note that it is also in *my* human self-interest as a humanities-based scholar to challenge the dominance of quantitative research.) But I do want to point out the all-too-human factors that intervene between the actual research and its broader circulation. Just as academic publishing is prejudiced toward statistically significant research, the political, journalistic, and funding mechanisms tend to highlight strong effects.

Correlation does not imply causation

This snappy phrase is taught in all beginning research methods classes as a way to caution students against the seductive power of statistics. A statistically established connection between two experimental variables is called a correlation, which is a purely mathematical relationship. Once you start looking for such relationships between variables, you can find connections all over the place. Once you find such a mathematical relationship, the job for the researcher is to interpret what the statistics mean. Just because two phenomena may be shown to be statistically linked does not mean that one actually causes the other.

As an outlandish example, one study found that the American stock market fluctuated in synch with brain activity in laboratory rats (Marzullo *et al.*, 2006). Of course very few people would be tempted to believe that the caged rats are causing the stock market to go up and down (though this provides an opportunity for jokes about the sleaziness of stockbrokers). But in the case of more commonsensical correlations, researchers have to guard against making the leap to say that one variable causes another. A savvy consumer of research looks for other possible variables that might provide a more powerful explanation.

If a study finds that people who commit violent crimes tend to watch a greater number of violent films and television programs, this seems to imply some sort of causal relationship. But the statistics alone do not tell us which factor might be the cause and which might be the effect. Maybe the media influence people to commit crimes, or perhaps criminals simply tend to prefer watching violent movies to chick flicks. The statistics alone have no way of telling us which explanation is correct, though because we have heard about this relationship for so long, our first instinct is to believe that media cause violence. But perhaps neither of these factors explains the group's tendency toward violence. Perhaps income level is the crucial factor, with poverty increasing the likelihood of criminal behavior and a preference for action films. Maybe a particular parenting style more strongly determines this behavior, or a hostile attitude toward the opposite sex, or a higher sugar intake, or any of a host of factors. A correlation alone cannot do anything more than hint at a possible relation between two phenomena. It cannot make claims about causation.

A large portion of media violence research is based on correlations, and correlation studies are generally believed by researchers to be among the weakest methods of investigation. They are particularly useful for providing hypotheses to test more stringently using other methods. As noted above, researchers can subdivide the group into smaller groups, testing to see if other factors (such as income or any other possibilities) play a more vital role in explaining the connection, but they can only do this with factors they overtly measure. If they do not measure parenting style in some way, there is no way of telling if a particular parenting approach leads more to violence than watching television does. Also recall that the more times you subdivide the group, the more participants you need in the study, so if you want to examine multiple possible explanations, you will need significantly more resources.

Perhaps because there are so many possible confounding factors, correlation studies linking media violence to aggression usually report a very weak connection. Such studies can do little more than provide instructive hints about possible causes for behavior, and yet much of the work on media violence depends on correlations. Researchers understand the limitations of such studies, but when they are reported more widely these limitations do not get emphasized. The question that the informed consumer should ask when they hear about such studies is: what other factors might explain the reported link?

One person's violence is another person's aggression

One reason why media violence researchers use correlation studies is because an "ideal" laboratory test would be impossible. Imagine signing children up for a study, showing some of them a violent film and others a more "neutral" film, and then seeing which ones beat the others up! Imagine an institutional review board that would approve an experiment where children might get hurt. It is much more ethical to study correlations among naturally occurring populations, although these kinds of studies don't provide strong answers regarding whether media cause violence.

For obvious reasons researchers rarely do experimental work on actual violent behavior. Generally they study a slightly different concept: aggression. The difference between aggression and violence may seem like splitting hairs, but the move from one concept to the other involves a subtle sleight of hand. What counts as aggression? Shoving? Harsh words? Invading personal space? The definition varies from researcher to researcher, but most are a far cry from the kinds of violent acts we fear. Maybe those harsh words in a child will escalate to murder when he/she grows up, but maybe not. Yet when we hear reports on media and aggression, we frequently connect the dots mentally between such "aggression" and school shootings.

Probably the strongest consistent experimental finding in media violence research is that some people (not all) tend to behave more aggressively for a brief period of time after watching violent media. Again the question is: what does this mean? Researchers rarely examine the intent of such aggression, and intent is crucial to understanding human behavior. Let's say that a researcher watches a group of boys watching professional wrestling and notes how many of them give mock forearm smashes to each other afterwards. This is aggression by virtually any research standards, but how do we interpret this not very surprising and not very alarming behavior? One likely interpretation is that this is *play*, but quantitative researchers rarely seek to discover what the meanings behind the observed behaviors are. How much of media-induced aggression is meant as ironic, as fun?

Is the above experiment really about aggression at all, or is it merely noting that people tend to behave briefly under the influence of a film's mood? I am more likely to embrace my wife after seeing a romantic comedy with her. Does this mean that movies promote better intimate relationships? If so, why aren't there hundreds of studies about this phenomenon to rival the research on violence? Is this not the same (admittedly temporary) effect?

"Aggression" is a slipperier concept than you might imagine in these studies, but so is the other major variable: "media violence." What gets to count as "violence?" Is an anvil hitting a cartoon character on the head the same as a real live actor getting punched? How does fictional violence differ from real-life violence shown on the news? What is the line between "explicit" violence that shows damage to the human body and "unrealistic" violence that does not show its consequences? And how is it possible to come up with a measure of such violence, even if you divide these onscreen acts into categories such as "fictional," "cartoon," or "explicit?" Even if you do segregate media violence into more narrow categories (as many good researchers do), you still lump different things together. To do so is to treat all members of a category as the same.

If all depicted acts of violence had the same effect, then there would be no need to pay one director more than another for an action movie. After all, violence is violence, right? But there is an enormous group of artists and technicians (directors, editors, sound mixers, special effects artists, and others) who devote long hours to making sure that the violence in one scene has more emotional impact than in another. Such professionals are intensely aware of the many small decisions that contribute to staging an effective action scene. How, then, can researchers lump all the different degrees of violent action into a single unified category to be studied? Are researchers studying the possible impact of the violent act being depicted, or are they studying the effects of fast editing, loud sound effects, and blaring music?

While we are interrogating words, why not question what it means for media to "cause" violence/aggression? When Dylan Klebold and Eric Harris put on long black coats straight out of *The Basketball Diaries* and shot their fellow students in Columbine, what role did that film play in their actions? We will never know for certain, of course, but it is entirely plausible that *The Basketball Diaries* influenced the *style* of their real-world violence more than the motivation to kill. For generations, people have been using movies to gain hints about how to look, dress, and walk with flair. In this sense, onscreen depictions have clear influence on our real-world actions. But do they "cause" us to do things? Or rather, do they tend to shape the *form* our actions take, with other factors playing a larger part in motivating us to take the action in the first place? Do images cause a teenager to shave his/her head, or do they influence the appearance of how they express their rebellion?

Because films, television, and video games circulate so widely, they provide ample fodder for those looking for a sense of style. Because we see the obvious, omnipresent "effects" of these images whenever we walk down a crowded street, it is easy to fear the media's influence on more dangerous forms of behavior. And so when we hear news reports about quantitative media violence research or particularly vivid examples of individuals imitating violent media, it reconfirms our commonsense fears. Jumping to such conclusions, however, can lead to sloppy thinking, confusing the form of an action with its motivation, or the style of a depiction with its content. Quantitative research methods hold out the promise to disentangle one commonsense factor from another, but the complexities of real-world behavior are hard to separate.

Is that your opinion or the "right" opinion?

The fact that "everybody knows" media cause violence is one of the greatest challenges to studying whether it is actually true that they do. How do researchers know if they are studying the phenomenon itself or the widespread *belief* in this phenomenon?

Let's return to our scholar trying to do an experimental study on media violence. Researchers tend to like to use real Hollywood film scenes in their experiments because these best duplicate the normal viewing situation for most people. Hollywood scenes, however, are often jam-packed. If the researchers show a particular scene to people participating in an experiment, how do they know we are responding to the violence and not the smartass dialogue or the actors' looks or the buddy relationship? The researcher often takes a violent clip out of context, trying to narrow the film down to its violent content (though it is enormously difficult to separate the content from its film style). Imagine that situation: being shown violent clips and then being asked about their behavior. Of *course* people understand what the "right" answer is because "everybody knows that media cause violence." How do you know if you're measuring a socially held attitude about what "people" do or the actual individual's link between watching violence and violent behavior?

Media violence researchers can insert tasks between the film screening and the later questioning to disguise the easy connection between the two in the individual's mind. But how can one ever know if one is studying the widely shared idea of media influence or the actual influence itself? It requires careful, creative research. Let's take a favorite example of mine from my own field of emotion research. There is a theory called "facial feedback" that says that the position of your face can influence your emotional experience. Smile and you will feel a little bit better. This is a particularly difficult idea to test, however, because it is so intuitively obvious. Again, imagine an experiment in which a researcher tells you to smile and then asks you what emotion you're feeling. Stupid question! It's obvious what the right answer is. One of the most ingenious experiments I have seen tested this hypothesis without testing our attitudes on the effects of smiling. The researcher asked the person to hold a pencil lengthways in their mouth (putting the muscles roughly in smile position) and asks them to hold the eraser tip in their mouth (simulating a frown). After each, they determined if the person's emotions change. This approach allowed the researcher to study the facial muscles without involving the *thought* of a smile or a frown. (By the way, smiling does make you feel slightly better.) To separate two such closely tied phenomena requires a creative researcher indeed.

The widespread belief that media cause violence actually makes studying media violence one of the most difficult problems in social science. Quantitative research promises the possibility of separating observable, repeatable, real phenomena from commonsense (and perhaps misguided) beliefs, but of course research is conducted by humans who share those common ideas. Good careful attention to methods can help minimize the influence of such ideas on research, but these common ways still structure the way we think about and interpret this work. For example, the most common experimental approach to the question of media violence is to assign people randomly to two groups, show violent media to one group and "neutral" media to another (never mind how difficult it is to determine what "neutral" media are), and then test their behavior/attitudes. The people in the violent media group show a more aggressive attitude, while those in the neutral media group show a less aggressive posture. What could be simpler and more airtight? Media cause aggression.

But that conclusion doesn't necessarily follow from the data analysis. An equally valid conclusion (but one that's much more difficult to see, given our social attitudes) is that perhaps the "neutral" film calmed people down. Without a third group to compare, there is no way to tell which of the two explanations is correct, and yet researchers rarely see the need for an additional group. Because they see through the perspective of our shared attitudes, they rarely consider the opposite explanation (that media can calm) that is just as well supported by the experiment's data. Our common belief that media cause violence not only clouds the minds being studied, but it also inclines the researchers doing the studying toward particular kinds of interpretation.

The problems posed by such attitudes remind us just how difficult it is to examine something as complicated as human behavior. Even a simple question can be enormously complicated to examine because of complicated human motives. For instance, what could be simpler than standing outside a polling place on election day and asking people who they voted for only minutes ago? And yet such exit polls have quite a mixed record of predicting the actual vote tally for an election, even causing the 2000 presidential election to be called by newscasters in favor of Al Gore over George W. Bush, only to have the exit polls proven wrong once votes were counted. Poll numbers for Senator Jesse Helms consistently underestimated his showings at the polls, which many assumed was because some voters did not want to admit publicly that they supported a racist candidate. Even anonymous responses are subject to skewing toward social norms. I remember taking an anonymous survey when I was a naïve, innocent high school student. When the questionnaire asked if I had taken illegal drugs, I reported that I had done so, although (at that point) I hadn't. I didn't want to appear "uncool," although there was no way for my anonymous response to be traced back to me. Once you place human behavior within its social context, it is enormously difficult to trace through the tangle of motivations and attitudes to get at the actual causes behind behavior.

Every quantitative researcher recognizes the difficulties of doing good work and understands the difficulties laid out in this article. And yet they have faith: faith that—over time, using varying methods, studying different groups—they will arrive at something closer to a real explanation of the phenomena they study. As a disenchanted psychology major, I tend to see the obstacles between quantitative research and the Truth about media violence. I still believe that good research is possible in this area. I also believe that researching this question is one of the most difficult jobs in the social sciences. It is our job as consumers of this research to question its findings as they circulate in popular reporting. The educated person should look further beyond what "studies show."

Bibliography

Anderson, C.A. and Dill, K. (2000) "Video Games and Aggressive Thoughts, Feelings, and Behavior in the Laboratory and in Life," *Journal of Personality and Social Psychology* 78.4: 772–90.

Babbie, E. (1986) *The Practice of Social Research*, 4th ed., Belmont, CA: Wadsworth.

Cumberbach, G. and Howitt, D. (1989) *A Measure of Uncertainty: The Effects of the Mass Media*, London: John Libbey.

Douglas, J. and Olshaker, M. (1999) *The Anatomy of Motive*, New York: Scribner.

Federal Trade Commission (2000) "A Review of Research on the Impact of Violence in Entertainment Media," *Marketing Violent Entertainment to Children*. Online. Available HTTP: http://www.ftc.gov/reports/violence/Appen%20A.pdf (accessed July 1, 2008).

Freedman, J.L. (2002) *Media Violence and Its Effect on Aggression: Assessing the Scientific Evidence*, Toronto: University of Toronto Press.

Gauntlett, D. (1995) *Moving Experiences: Understanding Television's Influences and Effects*, London: John Libbey.

Jones, G. (2003) *Killing Monsters: Why Children Need Fantasy, Super Heroes, and Make-Believe Violence*, New York: Basic Books.

Marzullo, T.C., Rantze, E.G., and Gage, G.J. (2006) "Stock Market Behavior Predicted by Rat Neurons," *Annals of Improbable Research* 12.4: 22–25.

Surgeon General's Advisory Committee on Television and Social Behavior (1972) *Television and Growing Up: The Impact of Televised Violence*, Washington, DC: U.S. Government Printing Office.

Further reading

Barker, M. and Petley, J. (eds.) (1997) *Ill Effects: The Media/Violence Debate*, 2nd ed., London: Routledge.

Mittell, J. (2000) "The Cultural Power of an Anti-Television Metaphor: Questioning the 'Plug-In Drug and a TV-Free America," *Television and New Media* 1.2: 215–38.

Chapter 6

Role models and stereotypes
An introduction to the "Other"

If you did a media-related research paper in high school, chances are that your project was about stereotyping. You may have focused on negative images of a particular group or examined particular "role models" that provided an alternative to stereotypes. These two approaches seem to have very different aims: one laying out the problem, the other depicting the solution. And yet there are similarities deep within these positive and negative stereotypes, and this chapter will examine how these two images are part of the same phenomenon, called "Othering." In some ways, this chapter takes the opposite approach from the rest of the chapters in this book. Instead of taking a single common term ("identification," "realism") and multiplying that into more precise language, this chapter takes two seemingly opposite categories ("positive" and "negative" images) and combines them into a single idea.

Not only are there threads that connect positive and negative images, but there are also connections across portrayals of different groups. Regardless of which group you examine, there are certain common themes in what might be called "images of" criticism (images of women, African Americans, Southerners, Muslims, and so on). Negative depictions of minority groups tend to emphasize the same kinds of character qualities, which gives them a sort of interchangeability. This chapter points out some of these parallel strategies, all of which are part of creating "the Other." As we begin to see patterns in the way multiple groups are portrayed, it becomes less likely that these negative qualities exist in the actual groups. What is more likely is that these strategies have become part of a generalized toolkit for portraying people who are "different."

What do we learn by looking at the connections between positive and negative stereotypes? One reason to explore the notion of the "Other" is to break down the link between a group's images and its real characteristics. You may ask, "If there isn't some truth to these stereotypes, then why do we keep seeing them?" This chapter explores how such images are propagated. And while I believe that we should work for more, better, richer images of people in media, at the same time I want to recognize just how difficult this is. If "Othering" is indeed part of the basic toolkit inherited by mediamakers, then how do they go outside the toolbox? This chapter also examines some of the pitfalls of well-intentioned mediamakers attempting to create "positive" images. By situating stereotypes within the larger process of "Othering," I hope to open up a discussion on the difficult tradeoffs of making images of underrepresented groups.

"Us" and "them"

Every group is deeply invested in policing its boundaries. From high school cliques to nations, we are concerned with defining who gets to be part of the group and who is on the outside. One of the challenges for a modern nation such as the United States is to decide what it means to be "inclusive" while still maintaining a distinctive identity as "Americans." Every bit of mass communication offers an opportunity for us to renegotiate or re-solidify our boundary as an American society.

In fact, I just did a common but subtle little boundary maneuver in that last paragraph, one of the simplest but most powerful ways of defining a group with words. I used the word "us" as if it were clear who was being addressed: "you" the American. If you are reading this in a British or Argentinian class, you have just been subtly excluded in that paragraph. I did this to provide a little demonstration of the power of the words "us" and "you." I will try to avoid excluding people so blatantly in the rest of the chapter, but I also want to acknowledge how difficult it is for me to avoid some level of Othering in this book. When I chose to write this book in a less formal tone, I necessarily created a mental version of "you" the reader, and undoubtedly this creates a "them." For most chapters of this book, I hope that the more personal address works well. In a chapter about the importance of addressing "you" and "them," this tone creates problems. I'll admit that I can't find a way around these difficulties without totally changing the book, and so I leave it in your hands. The bright student should not only read this chapter for its content but also look for the ways that my words create an Other. Go ahead; be brutal. It will give you good practice in thinking critically about how media express meaning.

The tiny words "we," "us," and "you" have considerable rhetorical power. If you accept my words as being addressed to you, then you consider yourself part of the "us." If you do not, then you are part of "them." Consider the way that newscasters, advertisers, or politicians use such terms when they address their audiences: "Radical Muslims are out to destroy our way of living"; "If you want to save money on your income tax, listen to this offer"; "This next story will put a smile on your face." You don't even have to believe that the message is true. All you have to do is to accept that the message is aimed at you, and then you have accepted that you are part of the "us," the group being targeted by the message. You are one of the people whose living is threatened by "them" (the radical Muslims); you are a lawabiding tax-payer who nevertheless wants to pay less money to the government. If you reject the message's call (changing the channel because you hate mushy feel-good news stories), then you have not only rejected the call to feel part of the group being addressed but you also have denied yourself the possible pleasure of participating in the text.

Louis Althusser calls this simple but powerful process "*interpellation*." Interpellation is when a person accepts that she/he is being addressed. Althusser's example is a police officer yelling, "Hey, you there!" If you answer the call ("Yes, officer?") or if you flee, you are recognizing that you are the person the officer wants to see. You accept an identity not of your own making but one that the officer offers: You are a "possible suspect." This identity is imbedded in the language; it may not even fit you very well. Nonetheless, if you answer or acknowledge the call, you are at least temporarily and partially accepting the role being addressed. You may even feel a little guilty, wondering, "What did I do to attract the cop's attention?" even if you did nothing wrong. Those who do not respond to the cop's shout do not consider themselves under suspicion.

Louis Althusser (1918–90) expanded on the ideas of Karl Marx, arguing that the influence of economics was more complicated than Marx proposed. Althusser said that the various social institutions (the church, education, government, the family, the media, and so on) did not speak with a unified voice to promote the status quo. Although all of these are interrelated through ideology, no one of them controls the others (Marx thought that economic structures were the base that determined a society's foundation). These institutions are relatively autonomous, and so they can contradict each other in their zeal to promote their agendas. Althusser also argued that instead of discussing the "individual" (a Romantic notion of a whole person who has free will) we should focus on the "subject" (a contradictory position that tries to cobble together an identity from the various identities offered to us by society). See Althusser's "Ideology and Ideological State Apparatuses" for more.

Althusser's example is a fairly broad one, but our mass mediated society sends hundreds of much more specific "Hey, yous" to us every day. A 16-year-old may barely register hearing a commercial message that says, "Are you looking to refinance your mortgage?" but I listen because I accept "homeowner" as one of my identities. Such "Hey, yous" do not even have to be in words. A commercial that shows trendy hip young people hanging out together is clearly not trying to sell me (a boring middle-aged guy) anything. I let that message pass me by, not accepting its call. We make our way through the world, acknowledging some calls, rejecting others. Bit by bit this positions us in society as members of this group but not that one, or at least as wannabe members of a group. I may not be as hip as those young people in the commercial, but maybe I am nostalgic for my younger days, or I aspire to be part of a crowd that know each other so intimately. I can accept the commercial's call on any number of levels: "Hey, you, hip young person, person who likes feeling young, or person who wants to be in the in-crowd." The "Hey, yous" of mass media have to be both narrow and broad: broad enough to attract the attention of a sizable number of people, narrow enough so that people will recognize they are being addressed.

The flip side of this process of interpellation is the way that it also excludes. Mediated images are always particular; they show specific people and specific places. When I was growing up in a rural Southern small town, I recognized the intent of those commercial messages aimed at teens who just want to have fun. I also recognized that the actual commercial images of those funloving people looked nothing like me and my friends hanging out on a Saturday night. In some ways, I answered the interpellation of those messages. Of course I wanted to have fun. But in other ways, I saw how the message did not fit me. I recognized that I was a "them" and not an "us."

I do not want to overstate the impact of a commercial message I saw when I was 16; nor is this intended as a plea for you to pity me. We are not helpless pawns of media shaping our desires. But one of the media's most powerful strategies is the simple "*Hey, you.*" Over time, through the power of repetition, interpellation can send messages of who belongs and who does not. The power is not in the messages themselves; we filter out many messages that do not "fit" us, and the media are only one source of material for piecing together our identities. These images become important for our self-identities when we accept their call, when we say, "Yes, me!" to the "Hey, you!"

Whether it is accepted or rejected, a call through the media defines a particular version of "people like us." It also frames a "them," which we call the "*Other*." The Other is anyone who is not "people like us." As we shall see, the Other is an extraordinarily useful category in story-telling. If mainstream media tend to create protagonists who are in some way "like us," they also populate the world with Others who either oppose the protagonists or present alternatives to them. In this way a film or television program creates a system of values, with some being nearer to "us" and others being positioned as different. In the rest of this chapter, I will examine some of the more common storytelling strategies that link values with Othered identities.

I will begin by looking at the images of one particular group because these images so clearly demonstrate the broad outlines of Othering. American Indians present an interesting case partly because their images have such a long history in American popular culture, dating back to Revolutionaries dressing up as Indians to throw tea overboard in symbolic protest at the Boston Tea Party. Popular imagery of Native Americans has been around long enough to move through several dif-ferent phases. In addition, American Indians serve as a useful case study because imagination plays such a large part in our images of Indians. In real life, the American government systematically relocated most Indians from their various tribal homelands to reservations that were physically distant from most population centers. Since mainstream culture so rarely encounters real-life Indians, it is relatively free to configure what little it knows about Indian culture into characters that serve useful roles in narratives. This is Othering at its purest, with little need to be constrained by the reality of actual Native American life.

American Indian popular images can be condensed into a single, useful combination: the "*noble savage*." The noble savage displays both central tendencies of Othering: that Others are different from us because they are naturally better than us in some crucial aspects, and that they are less completely human than we are. Although one side of this Othering seems complimentary to the group and the other insulting, the two aspects are intimately linked. When we assume that the other is different from us in some key aspect, this can be either frighteningly repulsive or exotically attractive. The image of the "noble savage" cap-tures tendencies of Othering: creating an impossibly decent image or a repulsive repository of what "we" have rejected. In many ways, the "noble savage" image embodies our attitudes about many groups, not just Indians. In exploring these assumptions, we will be laying the foundations for a wide variety of Othering.

At the heart of much Othering is the idea that the Indian is somehow closer to *nature*. "We" may have lost much of our connection to the land because we live in a modern world whose technology and pace cut us off from a more "natural" way of living. We want the conveniences of this lifestyle, but we also recognize what we have given up, and "we" are nostalgic for a deeper connection with the land. For most of us, this does not mean selling our modern possessions and living in a log cabin. Rather, this nostalgia for simpler times results in weekend car rides to spectacular parks set aside for the modern citizen to reconnect to nature in small doses. But Indians (according to the image) have not made this break from the land. They are much more attuned to natural rhythms of day/night and the seasons, where we try to control those natural phenomena through technology. Their bodies are hardened through struggles to carve out their existence, where we must subject our bodies to machines at the gym to gain a similar physique. Therefore their relationship to their bodies is different; they "live in their bodies" more, while we surround ourselves with the mental and imaginative pleasures of media and cyberspace.

This connection of *body* to nature, viewed in a positive light, provides the "noble" half of the "noble savage" equation. This can be seen in the figure of the shaman, who uses a mystic connection to nature to open up older, richer forms of consciousness. Perhaps with the aid of natural hallucinogenics such as peyote we can also bypass our modern programming and find a New Age peace by following a spirit animal who will guide us on the shaman's path. Or such a connection to the homeland creates a stronger value on family than "we" have, encouraging Indians to value their elders' wisdom instead of hiding them in institutions designed only for the aged. And thus the "wise old Indian" figure speaks truths that we cannot see because our modern eyes have been blinded through overexposure. Such Indians understand the value of *community* that we have lost as we immerse ourselves in television and computer screens, isolating ourselves from each other. The tribe/community is the source of meaning for this Indian. Because the tribe is more important than the individual, such Indians are nobly willing to sacrifice themselves for the greater good of the community. Revisionist Westerns portray these noble Indians as peacefully existing on the land until they were forced to defend themselves from Westerners wielding superior technology. The imperial "we" overthrew the noble Indian in our desire to occupy their land, and we hope to reclaim a portion of the conquered perspective by paying visits to air-conditioned cinemas to see stories of simpler people.

This connection to nature can just as easily result in a horrifyingly hostile figure, the "savage" part of the "noble savage." Nature may be beautiful and picturesque, but it is also powerful and destructive, and so anyone connected so closely to nature is also drawn to violence.

Civilization, with all its tendencies toward alienation and weakness, has the distinct advantage of curbing our animal desires. A more "natural" life puts people more in touch with the beast within, making them a danger to society. This image of the Indian gives us the classic Indian enemy, who tracks their prey by seeing signs in nature that we cannot see and who shrieks inarticulate, animalistic war cries before savagely slaughtering "people like us." This Indian indiscriminately kills men, women, and children, taking a scalp as we would take a beaver pelt, further showing his lack of value for human life. This Indian brings not only the threat of death but also the threat of an unbridled sexuality, as the warrior rapes the captive.

Usually we picture this Indian savage in the mythic past, and in general it is easier for us to picture Indians in the past than existing in our modern world. We acknowledge that real Indians still inhabit the twenty-first century, though our imagery of them still gravitates toward premodern times and values. When we do think of more modern Indians, we think of drunken Indians releasing their primitive urges because they cannot hold their liquor as a civilized person should, or of Indians running casinos. The Indian casino further ties the modern Indian to *irrationality*, although here they are able to exploit the exploiter's greed for money by running irrational games of chance. This Indian is lazy, which is the flip side of being linked to natural rhythms. Rather than making rational plans to gain money honestly through work (as we teach our children to do), this Indian passively expects to be taken care of by the government like a child. This understanding of the Indian as *child* encourages us to take a parental role, making decisions in their best interest about where and how they should live.

Table 6.1 will help summarize some of the different values associated with "us" and with the Indian "Other." Of course no single image of the Indian embodies all these qualities, but, as we have discussed, these values are all related through the process of Othering. I have described the case of images of Native Americans in some detail in order to point out how these patterns form the basis for depicting many other groups. Consider the connection between portrayals of African Americans and Native Americans. We see images of young warriors who have been placed into segregated areas (the "hood"), where they travel in tribes ("gangs"), engaging in brutal violence in defense of their land ("turf"). They are irrationally attracted to shiny garish objects ("bling"), just as Indians foolishly mistook beads and trinkets for real value, just as children play dress up to look more like adults. They also are depicted as lazy, preferring to receive government assistance than to eke out an

Table 6.1 Comparing "Other" values with "our" values

The Other/"them"	*"Us"*
Nature	Modernity
Savagery	Civilization
Body	Mind
Irrationality	Rationality
Sexuality	Repression
Laziness	Industry
Childhood	Adulthood
Tradition	Progress
Community/group	Individual
Past	Present/future
Connection	Alienation
Place	Mobility
Relaxed time/rhythm	Regulated time/rhythm
Timeless wisdom	Specific knowledge
Simplicity	Complexity

honest living. Black urban culture is depicted as a "hang out" culture, often full of brazen display ("booty shaking") that reveals their sexual confidence. If the young black person lives through this harrowing world, then he/she has a chance to become wise. The "wise older Indian" (played by Graham Greene in *Dances with Wolves*) and the "wise older black man/woman" (played by Morgan Freeman in *The Shawshank Redemption* or Cicely Tyson in *Diary of a Mad Black Woman*) serves essentially the same purpose in storytelling.

Or consider similar patterns in the understanding of "women." Advertising emphasizes "softer" selling as the way to target women, with ads focused less on rational information and more on emotional appeals. The standard formula for making a Hollywood action film more attractive to women is to give the male hero a love interest, since women are assumed to be more interested in intimate connectedness. This emphasis on interconnection makes women different in business and public affairs, according to such imagery. A world run by women would be kinder and gentler, more attuned to the needs of family, and thus "nobler." It would be less driven, more focused on taking time to talk with others in the community. Women have this different perspective because of the distinct experience of their bodies, according to this way of thinking. They give birth and therefore are more connected to childhood; they are tied to monthly cycles that make them irrational; they are obsessed with how their bodies look.

We can see similar patterns in the Western depiction of Asian peoples as being intimately more tied to community and family than "we" are, even to the point of squelching individuality for the good of the whole. Such individuals are capable of unthinkable sacrifice (kamikazes, hari-kari) to preserve the community. When we look at modern Japanese business strategies, we see them as operating with a distinctive communal culture. More typically, we Westerners picture Asian culture as a culture of the past, emphasizing stories of long-ago China and Japan over modern times. Everyone in a martial arts film seems to be born with a body that can engage in spectacular kung fu, just as everyone in black culture seems to have an innate ability to dance.

I do not believe that all stereotypes are exactly the same. There is a particular inflection in each group's stereotype (such as an Asian's martial arts abilities and Italian Americans as mobsters). But much of that stereotype retraces the outline of the Other (the Mafioso's value on family and violence, for instance). The particularity of a stereotype is the remnant that is left over after you remove the generic Othering strategies (for more on generic Othering, see the Na'vi in *Avatar*, which mixes and matches various bits of native imagery).

You can go on with this exercise (and I encourage you to do so), finding ways that various real-life "Othered" groups reconfigure the set of values (positively and negatively) that are on the chart. At some point in this discussion, some of you may speak from your own experiences to say, "Wait a minute! The stereotypes are partly true! Black culture *is* about dancing! Women really *do* like talking about emotions more! Chinese people *do* believe in family!" and so on. What I would say to you is that Othering makes it difficult to see the truth of any of these statements. Since Othering tends to portray groups as noble and/or savage, this makes it hard for us to see any actual nobility or savagery in the group. It is hard to separate the actual behavior of real people from the images that circulate concerning their group. How do you know if you are seeing a real group characteristic or simply an example that is more vivid because it confirms what you have been taught about that group through Othering?

Media Othering is not so powerful that it overrides your real-life experience. If you have spent considerable time in Native American culture, your images of actual Indians will outweigh a more generalized notion of the "noble savage." But Othering does shape your experiences and your interpretation of them. Othered images have a kind of *magnetism*. If we see a real-life instance that confirms our image of the Other, we tend to give that example special attention. The Other draws confirming real examples to it like a magnet attracts iron. Isolated instances that do not fit the Othered image are not clustered together (just as a magnet does not attract glass), and so they tend to accumulate less weight. Over time you can gather examples of group members that violate the Othered image, and you can reject the attractive power of the Other. But the image of the Other does exert a force in our perception, not only over groups that we know little about but also over populations that we encounter. By seeing how generic Othering can be, you can guard against an unthinking understanding that women are more tied to community or African Americans tend to be more sexual. Seeing the Other as a broad social pattern (and not a collection of isolated stereotypes) helps us begin to see our own world more clearly.

Creating the evil other, creating the funny other

When discussing the ways that popular images create Others, it is all too easy to blame Big Bad Hollywood (BBH). BBH is perpetuating stereotypes and doing damage to the social fabric of the world's societies. If we could just get those greedy, insensitive producers in BBH to think more carefully about the images they distribute, then maybe we could have more positive images.

However, almost every mediamaker I have met does not fit this stereotype of BBH. It is, of course, hard to generalize about an entire profession, but the mediamakers I have met tend to be thoughtful and well meaning, which complicates the idea that changing the personnel will also change the institution. Othering is part of the language of storytelling that Hollywood uses every day (see Chapter 3). Regardless of who is behind the camera or writing the script, mediamakers confront similar narrative problems, and Othering can provide a useful solution in many storytelling situations.

Let's take a simple scene in which you (the mediamaker) want your hero to walk down a menacing urban street. There are many different ways to convey this sense of a frightening environment. You could use sound effects to startle your protagonist or lighting to create sharp, deep shadows. You can also put intimidating figures on the street. Making media always involves a command of the details, and so you would have to cast particular actors to lurk in those shadows. You would need figures that would instantly convey criminal intent through their body types, posture, hairstyles, and clothing. Of course, anyone can potentially be a violent criminal in real life, given the right mixture of genetic disposition and social environment. However, in this storytelling instance, you don't have time to show how a group of clean-cut suburban white kids became a gang of menacing toughs. These are not major characters with complicated backstories in your film. These are extras who are onscreen briefly, and so you probably would rely on storytelling shorthand. You tend to choose African American or Hispanic over white extras; young rather than old; male over female. If you do choose a racial mixture of tough characters, you probably would rely on other counterbalancing factors from the language of imagery. Your lone white boy would probably be roughly shaven and darker; your white girl might be leather clad and pierced, not dressed in pastels. You are not being intentionally racist or sexist. You are simply a mediamaker trying to do a straightforward job: make it seem briefly dangerous for your hero to walk to a parked car. This is your hero's story, not the urban youths'. In telling that story, you have fallen prey to the magnetism of the Other. You have unwittingly reinforced its long history.

We learn this history rather quickly through frequent exposure to storytelling situations such as the one above. I learned just how quickly we absorb the language of Othering when my four-year-old son and I played with Lego blocks together. We were playing a "good guy/bad guy" scenario, and my son confidently chose which of the two Lego figures was the bad guy. Since I am an academic who deals with representation, I asked him why that particular Lego character was the evil one. He said, "Because it's darker." In spite of my best left-leaning intentions to raise a child without prejudice, my son had learned his lesson from four years of watching children's media. The villain in cartoons is the character with darker skin, facial hair, and a deeper voice. If only it were this easy to spot the "bad guy" in real life! But the media do not present the real world; they show one narrative situation after another, each one relying on the language of imagery, each one based on the multiple mini-calculations of specific representation for specific storytelling purposes.

The mediamakers' job is to maximize the story's impact on the audience, and so the temptation is to use everything in their power to make the villain as reprehensible as possible. One way to examine the history of Othering is to look at the villains in film. The most effective antagonist, all other things being equal, is one that activates a *society's deep fears*. Two figures representing chaos served this purpose in the Western: the savage American Indian and the outlaw who did not obey the "code of the West." Spy films, war narratives, detective stories, and action movies often need dependably recognizable villains for their narratives to work, and such figures can be powerful embodiments of Othered values. As our society becomes more attuned to identity politics, it becomes more difficult to find a "hissable" villain figure who does not represent a valued important minority, and so the Nazi, the terrorist, and the redneck can serve the dependable purposes that Indians and the Viet Cong once did.

In many modern media the hero bears a strong resemblance to the antagonist because he/she needs some similar qualities (a loose interpretation of the law, perhaps) in order to defeat the foe. In such cases, you should pay attention to how the film draws the line between "us" and "them" because such media provide particularly good laboratories to experiment with the nuances of villainous Othering. Of course fictional media do not present reality; they give us a closed storytelling system with limited options for our sympathies. The hero may be reprehensible in absolute moral terms, but at least he/she is morally preferable to our other options in the film/television program. One of the best ways to make a morally shady hero acceptable to us is to surround him/her with characters who are *more* shady, more Othered. Although Kareem Said and Tobias Beecher in the prison series *Oz* are sometimes capable of violence and cruelty, they are not as sadistic as most of the other convicts in Oswald State Penitentiary. Having more violent alternatives makes Said and Beecher seem more "like us." Such media encourage us to make moral calibrations: which of these characters' qualities is worse? These villains and heroes negotiate between those qualities that are valued and those that are Othered. (See Chapter 3 for more discussion on morally preferable characters.)

Horror media, particularly those dealing with the supernatural, provide useful case studies in villainous Othering because filmmakers have fewer worries about their representations upsetting any group of actual humans (since there are no powerful pro-vampire or -zombie rights organizations). Certainly the undead are horrifying, but if filmmakers can combine these frightening figures with our real-world anxieties, they can create even more effective monsters. Robin Wood has argued that one can trace the history of modern American anxieties by looking at the progression of monsters in Hollywood horror films. When horror films emerged in the 1930s, the villains represented a vague sense of "European-ness" (without insulting any actual European immigrant communities—where the heck *was* Transylvania, anyway?) threatening the straight white (and rather boring) romantic couple. After World War II the focus changed to more internal concerns. Wood argues that the family becomes the source of our anxieties. We are afraid that we are losing our innocent children (*Rosemary's Baby*, *The Exorcist*) to forces outside our control, creating misshapen families (*The Texas Chainsaw Massacre*). Horror media can activate our fears of the mentally unstable, encroaching technology, border invasions by real-life (illegal) aliens, and so on. Add some zombie makeup and these social fears can be made into well-disguised but potent monsters.

The Other can be frightening; it can also be funny. In its aggressive form, the Other appears to have vicious claws, but if you de-claw the Other, his/her difference can serve as the butt of our jokes. In the classic setup of a comedy duo, the "straight" man is the one who is more like "us," and the "funny" one more easily fooled than we are. Comedies often depend on a violation of our role expectations, and so they can reinforce those expectations by showing us their opposite. For example, remember our imaginary scene involving a gang of toughs. Now cast the scene with little old ladies, and you have a comedy. In fact, this is exactly what Monty Python did in the classic sketch "Hell's Grannies." The whole joke of the sketch is the comic spectacle of a gang of grandmothers on a delinquent rampage. This provides a twist on the "straight" way to stage such a scene, reminding us of our stereotypes about age and gender.

Sitcom casts are configured to provide multiple opportunities for laughs, but often the biggest outsider is the one who gets the biggest laughs. Everyone on *Friends*, *Cheers*, and *Seinfeld* delivers punchlines, but these sitcoms also create systems where some characters are more "normal" than others. Ross and Rachel are usually savvier than the clueless Joey and Phoebe; Sam is more grounded than the lovable losers who populate his bar; and Jerry (in spite of his many foibles) is still astonished at Kramer's bizarre antics. Many points of difference can be positioned as the funny Other in a sitcom, from political conservatism (*Family Ties*) to nerddom (*Family Matters*). The same quality can be "like us" in one comedy and Othered in another sitcom, depending on the particular arrangement of elements. In *I Love Lucy*, Lucy's desire to function outside the home makes her the Other, and her Hispanic husband Ricky has the more "reasonable" attitude concerning the woman's place in society. One could easily imagine another sitcom that makes the heavily accented Ricky (or Apu from *The Simpsons* or Khan from *King of the Hill*) the comic focus.

This comic Othering cuts both ways. On one hand, the biggest Other is the biggest butt of jokes, and thus participates in a long line of denigrating humor (one of the clearest ways to see how Othering works across groups is the interchangeability of many ethnic jokes. You can usually substitute "Polack" or "Texas Aggie" or "Manchester United Red Army" into "blonde" jokes—and vice versa—without damaging their humor).[1] On the other hand, the comic Other is often the breakout star. Zany Lucy is the star of *I Love Lucy*, not her husband Desi Arnaz. Urkel the nerd is the memorable figure from *Family Matters*. It's fun to play the comic Other; by definition, they get to do the most outrageous things. Without these figures' blundering, there would be no plot to these sitcoms, and so the Other can be the most narratively important character in the series.

This comedy strategy has a long, checkered history dating back at least to the minstrel days of blackface in America. One of the reasons white performers darkened their faces was that it allowed them to act more freely than white people could in proper society. Blackface allowed them to make verbal mistakes, to be more sexual, and to behave like animals. It can be hard to break free from this history of Othering, even when creating a feel-good narrative about accepting Others. For instance, *Shrek* appears to be a world full of Others, from ogres to outrageously accented cats. But some Others are more Other than others. Ogres Shrek and Fiona are the "people like us," with Donkey serving as the more outlandish comic figure (with African American comedian Eddie Murphy providing a blackface vocal performance). Comic Othering, therefore, is tricky. Becoming an Other can distinguish you from the crowd; it can make you a star. However, the price of that stardom is that you become the "problem" that must be solved in each episode. Lucy must be put back into the home; Homer Simpson's reckless actions endanger his family, and Marge must restore things to normal. The logic of much comic storytelling depends on someone sticking their neck out far enough to be different enough for "us" to laugh at them.

"You're taking these jokesters far too seriously," you may be saying. "They're comedians, not politicians. What difference does Homer Simpson really make?" One of the main points of this chapter is that a television program or film does not exist in isolation from the rest of media history. Part of the "joke" of Homer Simpson is that the dumbest

---

1 "Aggies" are the mascot of Texas A&M University, which has a spirited American football rivalry with the University of Texas Longhorns. The Manchester United Red Army is one of the most notorious groups of soccer "hooligans," whose spirited support of the British football club contributed to physical brawls and riots, particularly in the 1970s and 1980s. "Polack jokes" (which portrayed Polish immigrants as unintelligent) circulated widely in the United States in the twentieth century, perhaps most famously in TV's *All in the Family*. The "dumb blonde" stereotype has a long history featuring Marilyn Monroe, Judy Holliday, Suzanne Sommers, and Lisa Kudrow.

member of the family is the father, the one who allegedly should "know best." Mark Crispin Miller has argued that we can trace a shift in the depiction of sitcom families from earlier days in which the child was the source of the humorous problem and the father brought the wise solution to the problem ("Ward, I'm worried about the Beaver"). In the 1980s Bill Cosby was the "funny man" of the family as well as the source of family wisdom. With *The Simpsons* we see a full inversion of status: the father is a buffoon and the children are savvier and hipper. The reasons behind this shift are complex, involving a marketing focus on youth culture, changing attitudes toward parental authority, and so on. But Homer Simpson's humor depends on this changing history of the father's image in American pop culture. The shift from the father as having attitudes "like us" to the father as "Other" is significant.

The other crucial point to make here is that whenever you put a figure into a story, the relationships become complex. I have briefly cited Lucy Ricardo and Homer Simpson as relatively straightforward Others, but when you actually look at the narratives, these characters become more complicated. Yes, Lucy is the comic spectacle that her husband Ricky must tame, but there are times when Ricky is Othered for his funny accent and Lucy is more "like us." Similarly, Homer is the butt of many jokes, but there are times when the narrative positions him as more "like us," compared to Apu's foreignness.

Even while depicting these characters as "Others," these programs also gain sympathy for them by encouraging our identification, linking us powerfully with them (see Chapter 3). Narrative is complicated in the way it engages our social attitudes and our personal emotions. Rarely is a figure nothing but a "father" or an "Indian" in a narrative because the story gives them a particular history, and we can engage with various parts of the character. We can find simpler examples of Othering in briefer media forms, such as print advertisements and television commercials. In such short ads, we may see figures that purely stand in for "father" (as a man romps with his baby in a diaper commercial) or "Indian" (in an environmental public service announcement). These "characters" are meant to evoke their social type quickly, since the advertisement does not have time to give them particular backstories (we don't know how the father was treated by his father, or if the Indian sued to regain tribal land). Even the images in brief ads or in music videos can be complicated, particularly if they present stories. But the nonnarrative three-minute music video is probably the longest media form that can situate people mostly as "type." With anything longer than this, Othering becomes more complex because of the way that storytelling complicates character and elicits emotion.

The burden of the "positive" image

"Ok, even if you can't step outside the long history of negative images, you can certainly create positive images today, right?" Part of the difficulty in this question is the very idea of "positive" and "negative" images. Much popular debate about media forces this binary choice: is a character/celebrity a "role model" or a "negative/false image?" Such simple choices may make good fodder for pop articles, but they do a disservice to the complexity of storytelling. In this section we will discuss the hopelessly high standard of creating a "positive" image that is not simultaneously "negative" in some ways. We will discuss how the very idea of a "positive" image places an impossible burden on representations of the Other.

What would it mean for a character to be a "positive role model" for an Othered group? What would it look like if a single character was the positive embodiment of, say, "the black experience?" For this to occur, we must first believe that there *is* such a single thing as the black experience. What is the center of the African American experience in America? The obvious answer would be skin color, but "blackness" incorporates a large range of skin tones, and people with similar skin tones can think of themselves as either "African American" or "multiracial." One might say that discrimination is the centerpiece of black experience, but overt discrimination is a less prominent feature of a growing number of middle-class African Americans. Perhaps "black culture" (the church or African American music forms) is the factor that ties together the diverse people who consider themselves to be African American, but black cultural forms are also the backbone of mainstream culture. It is impossible to imagine American popular music without black idioms. How "black" is rap when the primary purchasers of rap albums are young white men? As Stuart Hall once asked, "What is this 'black' in black popular culture?"

Stuart Hall (born 1932) is one of the leading figures of British cultural studies, a school of thought that developed at the University of Birmingham, a city with (then) a vibrant industrial working class. Cultural studies says that any cultural phenomenon must be studied from multiple perspectives in order to understand it fully. The traditional university is structured into departments that encourage specialization, but cultural studies encourages scholars to work across these disciplines so that research will not be too narrow. Hall is known for emphasizing the active negotiation over meaning in culture. Instead of audiences passively swallowing the meanings encoded by an author, real audiences/readers take a variety of positions. Real audiences/readers can give the reading preferred by the author, or an interpretation opposite to the author's, or a variety of negotiated stances in between. Hall continues to write on culture, race, and identity. See *Representation: Cultural Representations and Signifying Practices.*

One of the fantasies of Othering is that there is a center to the Othered group. This can be a politically useful strategy; it can be advantageous for a group of people who call themselves "black" to act together as a political or economic unit. In such circumstances, it is useful for them to proceed as if there was a clear "essence" to blackness. But it is difficult to say exactly what the central experience is that links them all. The trouble with saying that there is a "center" to a cultural experience is that this also excludes other people as being "less central." There is a tendency to select a central "poster image" that embodies the Other. For lesbians, the white professional lesbian is the image that non-lesbians tend to picture when they think about the group. For contemporary black culture, the urban young man with ghetto "credibility" is the center. And so the urban "gangster" is "blacker" than a middle-class African American. His figure circulates more widely in black culture than, say, the rural black experience. A central image can help unite a community, but it also can divide that community with the now familiar game of "us" and "them."

It is impossible to find a single image that truly embodies a cultural experience, and so any high profile image of an Other is doomed to be inadequate. A character is necessarily a specific configuration of qualities. There is no way that this single character can depict the breadth of experience of people who call themselves "African American." For example, let us consider the most visible black man on television in the 1980s: Bill Cosby. In some ways, he played a seemingly perfect "role model" on *The Cosby Show.* He was an eminently successful doctor in an affectionate, mature marriage who presided over a loving family. His children presented problems, but he ably resolved them within each episode, fulfilling his role as classic sitcom father. In achieving this success, Cosby did not hide his black heritage on the show. He displayed Afrocentric art on the walls of his home, and he foregrounded black jazz musicians, who made appearances on the show. In almost every way imaginable, Bill Cosby, as Dr. Heathcliff Huxtable, portrayed a figure that black and white audiences could embrace. The problem with such a highly visible black "role model" was perhaps that it was so perfect that it was unrealistic. Although certainly there were successful black doctors in happy families in America, the portrait of the Huxtables was so far removed from the experience of many black Americans that it served as an unreachable fantasy.

Here we see the trap of the "positive image" of the Other. We want such images to depict qualities to which the group aspires. At the same time, we want them to be representative of the group's current state. How can any one image accomplish both goals? To err in one direction is to be "unrealistic" (see Chapter 2); going too far in the other direction can result in images that seem to continue negative stereotypes. We put impossible, contradictory pressures on images of the Other to stand in for all members of a group. We expect the black "role model" to embody the essence of the African American experience, if there is such a thing. To exalt any one figure as an example of the black experience is to make other black people's experience seem more marginal. The obligation to present a "positive image" is a heavy burden, forcing the weight of an entire group onto one character.

The tradeoffs in making "positive images"

Instead of trying to classify characters into two impossibly broad groups ("role models" and "negative stereotypes"), perhaps it would be better to discuss positive and negative *aspects* of such characters. Every character is a particular configuration of qualities, and often progressive characteristics are combined with more stereotypical qualities. But perhaps it is not enough to sort characters into "positive" and "negative," because any one aspect may have positive and negative consequences at any given moment in history. Rarely can progress occur without cost. Even a strategy that seems to represent a clear move forward is often tied to a tradeoff. Let's look at the tradeoffs of trying to advance the images of an underrepresented group.

In this section, I will survey some of the strategies that such mediamakers have used to depict African Americans. I have chosen African Americans because the large effort to improve such images over the last several decades allows us to see several different progressive strategies. Just as there are patterns in how media portray Others negatively, there are also patterns in how media try to make those images better. I will discuss these strategies in a rough chronological order, though I do not believe that progressive Othered images necessarily need to follow a particular order. By focusing on black images, we can see some of the tradeoffs involved in trying to improve representations of Others.

One strategy used particularly in early progressive images of Others is to make the Other the problem. This is the "*big issue*" strategy: placing the Other's difference at the heart of the narrative. When African

American Lucas Beauchamp is accused of murdering a white man in *Intruder in the Dust*, the entire story develops around the central question of whether the town's most prominent white lawyer will represent him, keep him from being lynched, and prove him innocent in court in spite of the odds. Beauchamp's race is the issue to be dealt with, not the question of his guilt or innocence, and a courtroom drama allows plenty of opportunity for making speeches about that issue. (We can see similar strategies in *Philadelphia*, where Andrew Beckett (Tom Hanks) is fired from his law firm only because he has AIDS, leading to a legal showdown.) The difficulty here is that the character at the center of these stories becomes synonymous with their issue/problem. Beauchamp is defined by his blackness to a large extent, and Beckett *is* his disease, as far as the narrative is concerned. Real people are more complicated, and so you cannot reduce them solely to their race or their illness. In addition, *Intruder in the Dust* provides an example of other progressive Othering strategies. Here we see the *white savior* who intervenes and saves the day, a strategy that keeps the focus on the issue but also seems to say that the Other is helpless to improve their own situation. (In *Philadelphia*, Beckett must convince a homophobic lawyer to represent him.) *Mississippi Burning* has a similar dynamic, with two white outsiders entering a tightly knit community to investigate a racially charged disappearance in the 1960s.

These two films, *Intruder in the Dust* and *Mississippi Burning*, also demonstrate another standard progressive Othering strategy: *setting the story in the past*. A civil rights story that occurs in the 1960s can provide an emotionally satisfying narrative where the forces of right defeat obvious villains (clearly racist Southern white men). Setting the story in "simpler times" does a disservice to the past (which is never simple), but it allows the narrative to be straightforward. It becomes easy for us to situate the problem long ago ("Racism was a big deal back then, but not any more"). Because such media depict racism using the familiar form of melodrama (with larger-than-life villains), they allow us to feel sanctimonious ("I am certainly not like that racist"). Situating the problem in the past (even when glorifying the historical struggles of real heroes) also allows us to be comfortably distant from any present version of the problem.

When the issue is the central focus of the film or television program, there is a temptation to "stack the deck," to make the Other so *impeccably good* that he/she cannot possibly be disliked. I call this the "Sydney Poitier" strategy. In *Guess Who's Coming to Dinner*, a young white woman brings home her black fiancé (John Wade Prentice, played by Poitier) to meet her old-fashioned parents. The shocked mother and father oppose the idea of the interracial union, but they are won over by

Prentice. How could they not be? Poitier's Prentice is "one of the good ones." He is an internationally respected doctor who is also a philanthropist. His manners are perfect; he is sexually chaste and financially responsible. The only thing you could possibly dislike about Poitier's character is that he is just too perfect. Again, the melodramatic formula tells us exactly how we should feel about this squeaky clean hero. The rationale behind this strategy is clear: make the Other so likable that the only possible reason to reject them is their difference. The tradeoff? By making our sympathies crystal clear, this implies that the Other needs to be flawless in order to be accepted. If the standard for acceptance is an Ivy League education, affluence, flawless social graces, and good looks, then how many real people can possibly achieve this? In trying to send a message of tolerance, such films can come across as setting the bar for acceptance impossibly high.

Another strategy (perhaps as a response to imagery of the Other who needs to be saved) depicts the Other as a *power fantasy*. During the Blaxploitation era of the 1970s, relatively inexpensive films such as *Shaft*, *Super Fly*, and *Coffy* showed black characters who literally kicked butt. These characters strode boldly and coolly through their worlds, certainly providing a figure of wish fulfillment for many black (and white) audiences. These figures were almost superheroic in their invulnerability as they quashed those who opposed them. Blaxploitation presented the anti-establishment version of this power fantasy, while the black doctors we have discussed (Poitier's Prentice and Cosby's Huxtable) present a version of the powerful African American who works within the system. The difficulty with these characters is that they appear fully formed and powerful; we have little sense of how they came to be this way. These characters appear to have taken an amazing leap to the head of the class in spite of improbable odds. Would the establishment allow a figure such as Shaft or Coffy in real life? How did Prentice and Huxtable gain their respected status? Such power fantasy figures can appear almost magical, as if they were somehow able to bypass effortlessly the structures that keep people from power. While identifying with such characters may give the pleasure of wish fulfillment, at the same time they can emphasize that this status *is* merely a wish, that it is unlikely for any one person to rise to these heights. Or such media can give the impression that our society has improved so much that nothing now holds an individual back from getting their wishes. It is easy to confuse images of power with real-life changes in the power structure.

Eventually, the figure of the "positive" Other can appear in a film without being the central focus of the narrative. In some ways this appears to be "progress," since the Other can appear as a "regular person" without being so disruptive to the story that they necessarily have to be the "problem." This strategy often results in the Other as *token*. Adding an African American to a group satisfies the overt need for "diversity"; adding more than one threatens to make the film/TV program appear to be targeted specifically at black audiences, not the "mainstream." The token strategy usually places the Other in a supporting role, not wanting to make the Other the protagonist and risk having audiences mislabel the text as a "black film" or a "black show." Others make great *"best friends"* to the white protagonists. In this role, they provide a listening ear when the protagonist has troubles to discuss, and often (in a variation on the Wise Old Black Person) they dispense savvy, sassy advice (Wanda Sykes has made a career out of such roles). This role integrates the Other into the mainstream community but keeps them out of the action that drives the narrative.

In this strategy, usually no one mentions the fact that the Other is actually Other, and this itself is an important strategy, called *"exnomination"* (literally, "not naming"). Exnomination is one of the most powerful ways to signal that someone is "like us." For example, look at the difference between these two sentences: "I have a friend who lives in that building" and "I have a black friend who lives in that building." The friend's race is not relevant to the discussion, and so the word "black" in the second sentence is extraneous information, or rather the race is not named in the first sentence. A white person saying this first sentence is probably doing exnomination; by not specifying the race, the assumption is that the friend is also white. By naming the race in the second sentence, the speaker is positioning the friend as "Other," as a member of a category that needs to be named. Richard Dyer has argued that part of the power of whiteness is that whiteness appears to be nothing at all. White people often do not think of themselves as white; they often think of themselves as having no race or heritage in particular. Exnominating their own race can free a person to "try on" another ethnic style, since their own race does not pose a barrier. This may enable a white person to dabble more easily in salsa dancing or Buddhism as a way to feel either more "passionate" or more "serene." For an African American to engage in Buddhist meditation may seem more a rejection of his/her cultural heritage. Exnomination can be freeing to the members of a group, but it can also subtly transform any group that must be named into an Other.

I recall a particularly consistent strategy of exnomination on the television show *L.A. Law* in the 1980s. When the show used a black actor as a trial judge for the first time, no one on the show commented on the actor's race. Having a black judge had no bearing on the trial (the case did not involve race), and so there was no story motivation that required the judge to be black. Though none of the other characters seemed to notice the character's race, I certainly did. "Wow! A black judge on TV! Cool!" I thought. The next time I saw a black judge on the show, I thought, "Wow, this show has some nicely progressive politics. They're putting African Americans on the bench." (Another way to read this strategy would be to ground it in realism, since there was a real-world push to increase African American presence in the judicial system.) Thereafter when I saw an African American presiding over an *L.A. Law* trial, I said, "Black judge" to myself. I named them. Eventually over time I stopped and simply labeled them "judges." At that point I no longer saw them as Other. Through a combination of exnomination and repetition, the makers of *L.A. Law* had made "progress," at least with me.

But as this chapter has made clear, progressive strategies of representation are difficult, and they change over time. When the same writer of *L.A. Law* (David E. Kelley) later did another legal show called *Ally McBeal*, the show also used exnomination in its portrayal of race and romance. When white Ally McBeal dated an African American man, there was never any mention of either of their races. Under these circumstances, the strategy that seemed progressive a few years earlier seemed like avoidance. How realistic is it that a white woman and a black man can have a long-term relationship without race having *any* bearing whatsoever? *Ally McBeal*, like most narrative texts, is complicated, but the point I want to emphasize here is that exnomination, like all of the progressive strategies I have examined here, has its tradeoffs, and that the meaning of any single strategy changes as the history of representation changes.

So what?

At the close of this chapter, you may be asking yourself, "Why should I care about images of the Other?" If you are a member of a minority group, you may say that you personally don't feel bound by the images that circulate of your group. Even if you do not think that images influence the real lives of group members, you should recognize the way that popular images create a forum for us to talk about the real lives of Othered people. When Murphy Brown had a baby outside of marriage, when Mel Gibson made anti-Semitic remarks, when we learned that Ronald Reagan's or Dick Cheney's daughter was gay: these images opened up moments where we could discuss what it means to be an unwed mother or Jewish or gay. If you do not think that the images are important in and of themselves, then you should at least recognize that we as a society behave as if they are important. We talk about and legislate images (such as those in video games) as if we were dealing with the real-world phenomena that these images represent. These fictional or celebrity images provide an opportunity for us to talk about the lives of real, ordinary, everyday people, and that discussion (like the one you have in your classroom) can have an impact that extends into people's lives.

If you are not a member of an Othered group, why should you care about this process, except for a general caring for other people's lives? Throughout history, groups have defined themselves by who they are not, and fundamental ideas take shape as we draw these boundaries. For instance, Orlando Patterson has argued that the way we know what "freedom" is depends on the practice of slavery. Whatever "freedom" means (and it means different things to different people), we know that it is not slavery, and so the opposite, the Other, defines the concept. Philip DeLoria has traced how we have defined the notion of "American" in reaction to our changing popular image of the Indian. DeLoria emphasizes that these images of the Other are not distant, separate concepts; in fact, one vital way we learn who "we" are is by playing the role of the Other. Throughout history, mainstream Americans have "played Indian": masquerading at the Boston Tea Party, reading *The Last of the Mohicans*, doing Indian crafts at camp, and going on New Age "vision quests." By doing these activities, by taking on Indian styles temporarily, by allying ourselves with Indian characters, "we" get a taste of what we think it would be like to be "them" before we go back to being "us." We can temporarily feel what it would be like to be a "gangsta" by rapping along with a hit single; we can inject more "passion" into our lives by learning to salsa or we can try on a bit of class by doing ballroom dancing; we can sample the exotic Orient for the price of a meal or a ticket to *Memoirs of a Geisha*. DeLoria points out that we *live* these images of the Other (at least temporarily on the weekends or in movie theaters), that we define who "we" are by sampling who we are not, and so the politics of Othering is not an issue solely for minorities.

Notice that the activities I just listed are not only things we do but also usually involve buying products. Although at one time these lived experiences may have required actual physical interaction with the Other, for most of us in the modern/postmodern world, these are commercial transactions. We pay for dance lessons, restaurant meals, song downloads, and movie tickets. Although these may feel like samples of another perspective, we should also remember that these perspectives have been commercialized, which necessarily changes them. A commercialized version of the Other is necessarily different from an "authentic" experience (if there is such a thing). It re-envisions the Other in a way that is more palatable to the intended audience, whether that audience is broadly defined (in a blockbuster film) or a targeted niche (the New Age audience). And so Cherokee Indians don full head-dresses to take pictures with tourists (although the feathered headdress is a Plains Indian tradition), and Chinese restaurants in Western countries cater to our expectations of what "Chinese food" is, often serving different menu items than the food consumed in China.

Popular culture has its own mechanisms that interact with but are separable from the rest of the "real world." Once it finds a popular image, popular culture tends to *recycle variations on a theme* until economics forces a change. Pop images can circulate for a long time with little connection to anything "real" other than other images. For instance, the fantasy of the Southern plantation continues to recycle imagery defined by romanticized stories written around the Civil War era, even though these images had little to do with the majority of Southern farms. As long as there is a market for the images, Hollywood will be tempted to perpetuate them, regardless of whether they portray a "realistic" vision of a group. Othering is something that groups throughout history do; this practice is given a particularly commercial spin in our time, which alters that process.

And so you cannot necessarily argue backward from the image to the real group. It is tempting to say that there must be some truth in these images of black people or American Indians; otherwise, why would they still be around? The answer to that question has to do with media's tendency to recycle images as long as they are commercially viable, as long as they satisfy some paying customers' fantasies. In our world, Othering is not only part of the language of imagery; it is also a fairly dependable way to make money, and that economic pressure helps explain why we continue to produce such images.

Throughout this chapter I have emphasized how difficult it is to represent the Other. I believe that the categories of "positive" and "negative" images are not helpful for discussion because actual images are so much more complicated than this artificial binary. We do a dis-service to both the images and the group being represented by pressur-ing images to bear the burden of providing a "positive" representation. No one image can stand up to such pressure.

And yet I do believe that it is possible for us to make "progress" in representing the Other. Over time we can hope to widen the range of representations from the "noble savages" favored by popular culture. No single image produced will be unabashedly positive, even if it is made by a mediamaker who belongs to that group. No mediamaker (whether Othered or mainstream) can fundamentally reinvent the language of imagery that they inherit (see Chapter 3 for more on this idea). My hope lies in broadening the range of representations of the Other and in the process of repetition. It takes time to reshape our conceptual categories, and this requires changes in both the quality and quantity of images of a group. Popular images are only part of how we construct our categories, of course, and our real-world interactions with Others also play a large role. But popular imagery's participation in this process can be improved if we see a wide range of characters (from villains to heroes, from bit players to protagonists) repeated across a broad variety of media. Over time, using a variety of strategies, these admittedly imperfect images of the Other have the potential to overcome the magnetism of stereotypes to create a richer, more nuanced portrait of our world.

Bibliography

Althusser, L. (1971) "Ideology and Ideological State Apparatuses," in *Lenin and Philosophy and Other Essays*, New York: Monthly Review Press.

DeLoria, P. (1999) *Playing Indian*, New Haven: Yale University Press.

Dyer, R. (1997) *White*, New York: Routledge.

Hall, S. (1993) "What Is this 'Black' in Black Popular Culture," *Social Justice* 20.1–2: 104–15.

—(1997) *Representation: Cultural Representations and Signifying Practices*, London: Sage.

Miller, M.C. (1986) "Deride and Conquer," in T. Gitlin (ed.) *Watching Television*, New York: Pantheon Press.

Patterson, O. (1991) *Freedom: Freedom in the Making of Western Culture*, New York: Basic Books.

Wood, R. (1985) "An Introduction to the American Horror Film," in B. Nichols (ed.) *Movies and Methods*, vol. 2, Berkeley: University of California Press.

Further reading

Dyer, R. (2002) "The Role of Stereotypes," in *The Matter of Images: Essays on Representation*, 2nd ed., London: Routledge.

hooks, b. (1992) "Eating the Other," in *Black Looks: Race and Representation*, Boston: South End Press.

Lott, E. (1995) *Love and Theft: Blackface Minstrelsy and the American Working Class*, New York: Oxford.

Neale, S. (1993) "The Same Old Story: Stereotypes and Difference," in M. Alvardo, E. Buscombe, and R. Collins (eds.) *The Screen Education Reader: Cinema, Television, Culture*, New York: Columbia University Press.

Williamson, J. (1986) "Woman Is an Island: Femininity and Colonization," in T. Modleski (ed.) *Studies in Entertainment: Critical Approaches to Mass Culture*, Bloomington: Indiana University Press.

Part III

Discussing media's future now

Chapter 7

What difference does a medium make?

In Chapter 5 we looked at the broad conversation on "media effects," at society's discussion about how television has allegedly made our attention spans shorter or how video games can possibly cause more aggressive behavior. I emphasized the "effects" portion of that relationship, suggesting that we should question whether studies actually "show" such links clearly. In that chapter I did not question the other side of the equation: the concept of "media." This chapter asks you to think about exactly what a "medium" is.

This may seem like the silliest question this book has proposed thus far. Of course you know what "film," "television," and "the internet" are. You can point to your television set sitting in the corner, and you access the internet through your laptop. But in what ways is the internet a "medium?" What is a "film," exactly? Is "film" defined by what we watch or where we watch it? If we watch *The Lord of the Rings* on a computer or cell phone, does that make it any less a "film" than if we saw it on a big theater screen?

Technological convergence has certainly blurred the boundaries among our concepts of "media," but this chapter will argue that the notion of a "medium" was never so clear. We have a tendency to assume that a medium is defined by its physical architecture, that the actual hardware is the same thing as the medium. Reducing the medium to its technology may make things simpler, but this also can cause some sloppy debate. People who assert that "television" is harmful often will specify that certain television shows, such as *Sesame Street*, are beneficial for children, as if *Sesame Street* were somehow not "television." We debate whether the internet is destroying our sense of community by isolating each of us in front of our own personal screen, but that debate usually depends on thinking of the internet as a single entity. Is "the internet" one thing, or is it several different media? By looking at the hardware, do we misrecognize what the "internet" is?

What difference does the definition of a "medium" make? One important reason is that our society makes rules about media, or rather we make regulations based on discussions of what we imagine those media to be. Instead of talking about actual media, policy debates often center on our common understanding of what a medium is. When we discuss "television" or "the internet," we have a shared sense of what we mean, but that rarely involves the full range of content on the television or computer screen. Usually such discussions focus on a very particular subset of the medium, and we legislate based on that. Our assumptions about the nature of the medium may allow us to simplify our policy discussions, but one of the purposes of an introductory media class is to help you see the complexity of the current media landscape. Going beyond the simple equation of hardware and medium will help you to spot sloppy thinking, both in private conversation ("television sucks, but I love *The Sopranos*") and in public debate ("the internet is separating us").

The essence of a medium

If we treat the hardware and the medium as if they were the same thing, then *technology can appear to define its own destiny*. It is easy to accept television in its current form as if it were natural, as if the structure of television programming were an inevitable byproduct of the basic nature of television itself. The key to understanding television, according to some, is that it is a domestic medium. Because it is viewed in the home, we necessarily interact with it differently than we do with the public medium of film. Audiences in a film theater are supposed to sit quietly, but many TV viewers tend to engage in domestic tasks (chores, family arguing) while watching television, and so we divide our attention between the screen and our household duties. According to this line of argument, television mirrors the structure of domestic work, which is full of interruptions (telephone calls, children crying). American television narratives themselves are frequently interrupted by mini-stories called "commercials," and storytelling must be designed around this structure, including plot "hooks" just before the commercial and repeated plot summaries (in case distracted people miss important information). "Watching TV" (in this scenario) involves watching the images "flow" from program to commercial and back again for long periods, until the overall experience of TV viewing becomes more important than watching a single individual program. This household storytelling situation encourages the viewer to interrupt television further, channel switching to create their own personal "flow" of images, making the television experience even more disjointed.

British theorist Raymond Williams described the experience of American television as "*flow,*" as a stream of images that smoothes over any interruptions and contradictions. Not only do commercials disrupt and oppose the TV program's narrative, but the TV narrative itself tends to jump around and contradict itself. When you sit down and watch "whatever is on," you are watching flow (as opposed to selecting a particular program to view). Williams's concept has become one of the most influential ways of thinking about television before video recording.

Television is "dumb" (according to its harsher critics) because it must appeal to this distracted viewer. Such critical voices often cite this distracted/interrupted "property" of television as being particularly harmful, arguing that we are now less capable of linear thinking because television's interruptions have "shortened our attention spans." Because television is in the domestic space, its basic property is interruptibility, which inclines TV toward trashy sensationalism that makes short, snappy appeals to the "least common denominator" (as opposed to the longer, more mature form of the novel).

This line of argument proceeds out of assumptions that television is domestic technology and that this technology is naturally supported by commercial advertising. After all, that's what television is, right? Similarly, influential media prophet Marshall McLuhan argued that our engagement with television depends on the way television makes images at the most basic technical levels. Television produces moving images by sequentially scanning rows of pixels (which you can see if you stand close enough to a standard television screen). There is no such thing, therefore, as a static "image" in television (unlike the single frames you can see when you look at a strip of film). The television image is constantly being remade pixel after pixel (which causes its "flicker"). McLuhan argued that our interaction with television was grounded in this physical property. Television elicits our participation in a distinctive way, since it requires us to make its imagery out of the component pixels. In McLuhan's terms, this makes television a "cool" medium that requires us literally to fill in between the lines, as opposed to "hotter" media (such as film) that show us detailed, solid images that do not require quite the same basic level of participation. Because of this fundamental property of television images, McLuhan could argue that the medium itself was more important than any particular content on television. In his evocative phrase, "the medium is the message," not the TV programs themselves.

Marshall McLuhan's widely read books of media theory (*Understanding Media, The Medium Is the Message*) made him a popular intellectual celebrity in the 1960s and 1970s. He believed that new technologies (from print to mass media) brought about fundamental revolutions in consciousness. McLuhan focused on the cognitive and sensory tasks required by the medium itself, arguing that these patterns of media participation powerfully shape our thinking. McLuhan prophesied that contemporary mass media technologies would transform the world into an updated version of the tribal village. By interconnecting people across national boundaries, modern media would create a "global village" for exchanging ideas.

Thinkers like McLuhan who ground their understanding in the medium's hardware inevitably believe that a medium has an "*essence*," that the particular medium does some one thing better than any other. This idea has a long history, that each new medium changes the previously existing media, freeing them from the burden of realistic representation, liberating the older media to do what they do best. Painting used to be the primary way to capture a realistic image of a loved one, but when photography was invented the new medium took over this responsibility, since it could capture the world more accurately and easily. This altered our understanding of what painting "should" do. Instead of trying to present a "true" picture of reality (which painting could never do), artistic painting changed to emphasize the "essence" of the medium: the brush stroke. Instead of hiding the paint stroke to create a realistic portrait of a flower vase, much modernist painting made "paint" and "color" the focus of their work. Painting foregrounded the artist's interpretation, not the artist's faithfulness in copying the world. We go to see Van Gogh's *Starry Night* not to get a better glimpse of the night sky but to see how Van Gogh uses paint to provide his own idiosyncratic interpretation of the stars. Van Gogh emphasizes that paint itself is the essence of the art of painting.

When film emerged, the practice of photography changed in ways that made its "essence" clearer. Photographer Henri Cartier-Bresson believed that photography had the advantage over all other arts in showing us what he called the "decisive moment." A good photographer captures action at its most expressive moment, freezing it in such a way as the naked eye could never see (capturing a runner hovering in mid-stride over a puddle, for instance). Snapping a picture at this decisive moment emphasizes the quality that distinguishes photography from motion pictures: its stillness. Photography cannot capture motion, but this does not make it inferior to film; instead, its stillness becomes the expressive essence, the thing that photography does best.

Similarly, the arrival of film changed theater. Theater, the dominant visual storytelling medium for centuries, lost this status to film because of the cinema's greater realism and its mass distribution. This freed theater to emphasize what it does best: live acting. Each theater performance is different from all others, and so the theater's distinguishing factor becomes the live presence of the actor, which film cannot duplicate. Theater provided live actors throughout its history, but film helped clarify that this was theater's distinctive selling point. Similarly, the comparison between film and television suggests that television's distinguishing characteristic is its ability to broadcast live, potentially uniting a country or the entire world as we watch the same images together. To this way of thinking, comparing one medium to another helps us see each medium's true essence.

Viewed in the abstract, media essences make a great deal of sense. You hear this concept when the local television news proclaims that it's "live!" Such ideas have inspired artists to create new works that take advantage of these essences, such as Jackson Pollack's "action paintings," where he splashes and spills paint on large canvasses in ways that try to convey the activity of painting to the museumgoer. But as Noël Carroll asks, what is gained by thinking a medium has an essence? If a medium has an essence, then this creates a hierarchy, with some forms of film/ television (for instance) being more "cinematic" or "televisual" than others. But what do we gain by saying that certain novels would make better film adaptations than others (a John Grisham novel over a James Joyce work, for instance)? What is the advantage of saying that certain kinds of artistic technique are more valid uses of the medium than others? Doesn't this discourage artists from making a full range of art, enthroning certain kinds of tastes as being the kind of art that "should" be made and seen?

Jackson Pollock (1912–56) was a leading figure in Abstract Expressionist painting. Instead of carefully applying brushes to a canvas placed on an easel (as most traditional painters do), Pollock experimented with bold splotches of paint that he poured, splattered, and dripped onto large canvasses on the floor, creating abstract works with an improvisational feel. Pollock himself was an intensely private figure of volatile passions, which he appeared to express through his "action paintings."

The idea of a medium's essence also does a disservice to the medium's history. A medium often takes a more complicated path of development instead of moving toward some preordained "essence." Radio, for instance, began as an outgrowth of the telegraph, as inventors worked to create "wireless telegraphy" that would allow people to send individual messages from point to point without needing to string cables. The "defect" of wireless telegraphy was that you couldn't keep the messages private; they could be overheard by many listeners. This liability (according to its original conception) became part of the joy of early radio, as amateurs created a community of users who chatted and listened to far-flung conversations. Some amateurs began to play records on their radio transmitters, repurposing a medium of communication into a medium of entertainment.

In the 1910s radio was a hobby practiced by technologically savvy amateurs who loved its unlegislated frontiers (much as people today argue that the internet should be open to all). By the end of the 1920s, the medium had been taken over by commercial networks, thanks to federal legislation that pushed the amateurs to a narrow portion of the radio spectrum. "Radio" in America then became synonymous with what we now know as "commercial broadcasting." Networks (adapting a structure from newspapers and magazines) interspersed advertisements with feature stories and entertainment programs. A distinguishing selling point for these radio broadcasts was their "liveness," with radio performers perfecting an intimate, sometimes improvised style in addressing the unseen audience. One could also argue that the essence of radio was in how it called upon audience members to use their imaginations. Unlike film or theater, which presented stories by showing us places and people, network radio storytelling encouraged people to create their own mental pictures of characters and exotic locales.

Radio radically changed once again when networks abandoned it to create a more profitable medium: television (inheriting an essence of "liveness"—along with the basic form of commercial broadcasting— from radio). Without programming feeds from networks, local radio stations needed a cheap source of material to fill airtime, and they found the answer in "disc jockeys" playing records. Radio became the opposite of "live"; it played recorded music instead of staging live theatrical productions or concerts, giving American radio the primary format it still uses today, where "radio" can be heard via satellite on television systems or as streaming audio through computer systems.

Where is radio's "essence" throughout this history? At times the medium was a wide open amateur playground; at others it emphasized the way its live commercial broadcasts activated the listener's imagination. At other times it abandoned storytelling to focus on music. To choose an "essence" is to stop history's motion at a particular time, as if the dominant practices at that moment defined the medium. In addition, such an account makes the progress of a medium appear natural. There is nothing "natural" about commercial broadcasting, although Americans now are so familiar with the form that they accept it as inevitable. Powerful hands (from large corporations to government regulatory agencies) shaped the history of radio into its commercial form, and powerful hands (including record companies) reshaped it into a vehicle for promoting record sales. Discussions of a medium's "essence" tend to leave out the struggles among competing interests and visions in a medium's history, encouraging us to accept the end product of that history as being preordained.

What is an invention?

A medium's history involves a struggle between alternative visions, even in the beginning when the medium was nothing but an idea. In a medium's "prehistory," it is not apparent what the technology being developed will do. When people were trying to invent the motion picture, what did they have in mind as the eventual goal? Certainly they did not envision the massive coordination of technological and artistic effort required to make a major blockbuster film. Many thought that motion pictures would be used for scientific purposes, not for entertainment. Eadweard Muybridge and Jules Marey used film to create "motion studies" that would help researchers analyze the movements of humans and animals. These early pioneers thought of the camera as something comparable to a microscope or a telescope: a scientific instrument that allowed us to see things in the natural world that the unaided eye cannot perceive. Marey's camera-gun captured the action of bird wings in flight, and Muybridge's successive photography answered the question of whether a horse picks up all four hooves at once when galloping (it does). How different the history of movies would be if this scientific vision had become dominant! What if early filmmakers hadn't decided that the real world was too unpredictable to capture efficiently, causing them to turn from the most popular films of the end of the nineteenth century (early documentaries) to a more predictable format: fiction (where our actions can be repeated for cameras, unlike historical events)? In this alternate future, would documentaries dominate the local theater? Would film cameras be used in biology classes as a scientific instrument like a microscope?

Marey's and Muybridge's scientific instruments did not produce moving images projected on a screen. So could these really be called "motion pictures" or "movies," or were they "pre-inventions" of the movies? What exactly is an "invention," anyway? Brian Winston has argued that an "invention" is not merely a combination of technology and ideas. Ideas and technology can create (in Winston's terms) "*prototypes*," functional machines that have not yet found a clear function to serve in society. To transform into a true "invention," a prototype requires a "*supervening social necessity*," a broadly held need that the invention fills. One way to think about this idea is to consider various innovators to be nominating their new technology to the society, waiting for the broader culture to endorse a particular form of equipment by broadly adopting it.

Thinking of an invention in this way helps to explain how technology is adopted. Many designers create machines to serve purposes, but if those machines do not meet a broadly held need, these prototypes function more as gadgets than as widely adopted inventions. If a prototype manages to do a "good enough" job to satisfy a partial need, then this technology can actually delay the development of the invention that eventually satisfies the major need. For example, the correctable typewriter performed adequately enough at creating print documents, thus alleviating (for a while) the need that was eventually solved by computer word processing. There is no guarantee that the society will endorse the best made, most innovative technology because the "necessity" being met is not always clear. For example, when video cassette recorders became commercially available, consumers were presented with two formats: Betamax (which produced a superior image) and VHS (which enabled people to record longer on a single tape). After a brief format war, society chose the VHS system. Surprisingly, the quality of the image was not a major factor in society's necessity; the recording capability became the dominant necessity (somewhat illogically, since people mostly watched prerecorded videos instead of programming their machines to record).

Inventions do not necessarily match a pre-existing need that exists in the society, waiting for the right technology to fulfill that necessity. Sometimes the "need" for an invention is something that is created. This new necessity can be produced by other technology (railroads created the need for the telegraph to coordinate rail traffic, for instance). It may be produced by a corporation's drive for profits. For example, there was no broadly expressed desire for digital recordings of music, even though compact discs could produce a cleaner sound without the pops and hisses of vinyl records. CD sales lagged until the music industry (having saturated the market for records) decided to stop making vinyl records, thus suddenly creating a "need" for compact disc recordings (and allowing the record companies to make new profits on old product.

When turntables became obsolete, this forced people to buy digital copies of albums they had previously purchased on vinyl).

Of course corporations are not all-powerful entities who can use the media to make us want things, though we sometimes talk about advertising as if it had this power to sway people. Certainly there are examples (such as compact discs) where coordinated corporate decisionmaking resulted in a newly created "necessity," but there are many more examples of products that have languished on the shelves in spite of huge media campaigns to create a need for them. For Winston, "inventions" involve a negotiation between producers and society, with neither one having total control.

Paul DuGay *et al.*'s case study of the design and distribution of the Walkman (Sony's influential portable music player) shows how consumers use media in ways that the inventors never envisioned. Sony never imagined that people would use the portable system as a source of literature (through recorded books). Nor did they dream that Chinese youth would use these private stereo systems as a way to connect to music that was not approved by the authorities. In China the Walkman became a political force that fed youth rebellion in difficult times. Although designers created the technology with a clear need in mind, the technology's purpose is never clear till it is placed in a social context.

If we think of an "invention" as a negotiation between technological implementation and social adoption, this allows us to explain better the idiosyncratic history of a medium's development. For instance, it was not initially clear what "television" would look like, what particular necessity the technology might fulfill. Perhaps TV would be used to send copies of documents (the principles used to create television are roughly the same ones used to scan, transmit, and print a fax). Television's development (in its current configuration) was sustained by various long-term factors and needs (the desire for realistic moving images, the industrialization of mass entertainment, the reorganization of the American home around the nuclear family), none of which was enough to bring about its full invention. Partial prototypes (machines that worked but not very well) slowed its invention (mechanical television became a dead end, distracting inventors from the eventual solution: electronic television). It was difficult at first to recognize that one of the necessary components of television was the cathode ray tube because that technology was used for physics experiments, not for transmitting signals.

Eventually the technology basically coalesced for television by the 1930s, but television still did not appear widely until the late 1940s and early 1950s. In Winston's terms, there were several supervening social necessities (including 1950s consumerism and postwar industrial capacities), but the primary necessity was the need for manufacturers to make television sets, having saturated the radio market. Television then looked to its predecessor medium (radio) for a model of how to structure its programming. In this erratic manner, a distinctive medium was invented, full of false starts and wrong concepts in development, incorporating elements from other media and technology, balancing corporate interests and social needs, but hardly guided by an abstract notion of the medium's "essence."

Borrowing and trapping fantasies

Another way to think about a medium is to recognize how media borrow from each other. Rather than seeing media as distinct entities whose unique properties lie within their technologies, we can consider a medium as a *hybrid blend of other media*. Television combined visual storytelling from film with the liveness and program structure of radio, which itself borrowed formats from magazines (TV programs such as *The Today Show* still refer to themselves as "magazines") and intimate patter from vaudeville. Film relied on a conception of "realism" (see Chapter 2) inherited from various media (photography, journalism, fiction, theater) and incorporated various storytelling techniques from the novel (character motivation and the linear cause and effect of plot) and melodramatic theater (including sensational cross-cutting between plotlines). Computer games incorporate the point-of-view shot and the fight scene from film; the quest narrative to gather powerful objects from the fantasy novel; and the skill levels/attributes from face-to-face roleplaying games.

No medium starts from scratch. Any new medium must have content, and the easiest place to find content is in existing media. Older media forms can provide familiar landmarks that help users navigate the unfamiliar territory provided by a new medium. The graphic interface revolution in personal computers involved organizing their data into "desktops," "documents," "folders," "mail," "rooms" for chat, streaming "video," web "pages," and so on (although computer users may now be more familiar with electronic folders than the paper file folders that inspired that term). In spite of considerable ballyhoo about "new media," much of "new media" often reconfigures older media. (See Chapter 8 for a discussion of new media and "interactivity.")

Jay David Bolter and Richard Grusin have used the term *"remediation"* to describe the representation of one medium within another, and a large part of remediation involves the tendency of newer media to reshape older forms. They also use this term to point out the reverse process: how older media often remake themselves to resemble newer media. The newspaper had established a familiar format through decades of publication, but when *USA Today* emerged in 1982, it remade the newspaper to include graphic elements and a less word-intensive style familiar to television news watchers. Computer users at the end of the twentieth century demonstrated that they were capable of monitoring immensely complex screen images (keeping track of multiple overlapping windows with various concurrent tasks), thus making the television format appear "flat" by comparison. TV producers responded by layering graphic images reminiscent of web content onto the more established television format, including news "tickers" that display rolling headlines, popups that promote upcoming programs, translucent "bugs" (icons that identify the network), and so on. Some modern theater productions (far from a sole emphasis on the live presence of actors) have integrated multiple projection screens into their stages. Commercial practitioners generally do not want their media to be considered "old-fashioned," and there is a pressure for more established media to compete with newer technology by incorporating aspects of the new medium's look. New media certainly sample from previously existing media, but older media also remake themselves by borrowing from newer forms.

We have discussed how some people have argued that a new medium refocuses the old medium on what it uniquely does best (for example, releasing painting from the burden of realistic representation). Others (including Bolter and Grusin) see a medium as a mix of components adapted from other media, a two-way process of borrowing between old and new media. Today we call this "convergence," which we can clearly see because media content crosses hardware platforms so readily. Looking at history shows us that media content has been crossing platforms for a long time, and that such borrowings can help create the fundamental "definition" of a new medium (television inheriting its "liveness" from radio, for instance). The boundaries among media obviously blur today, but those boundaries have been permeable for a while.

John Durham Peters has argued that the idea of a medium is a kind of trap, both for academics and for policymakers. On the one hand, we tend to have a misplaced faith in the medium's concreteness, paying too much attention to the physical medium itself. And so universities organize departments called "film" and "English literature" instead of "fiction" and "documentary," thus emphasizing the medium where the content resides instead of the cross-media continuities in storytelling. Academic publishers label their books "film studies," "television studies," and "new media studies" in their catalogs. American copyright laws are based on the actual medium of publication/transmission, and so live music performance (for example) has a different legal status than recorded music. Legal protections have to be extended to new media (film did not receive First Amendment protection until the 1950s), and regulations differ based on physical channel (the Federal Communication Commission historically has treated broadcast television networks differently from cable networks). We tend to treat "television" and "film" as if they were distinct, legislatable, observable entities, instead of studying "chat" (in online chat rooms, celebrity talkshows, face-to-face interactions, telephone calls, instant messaging), "gossip" (in tabloid newspapers, among friends, in forwarded email), "games" (TV quiz shows, board games, playground activities, bar trivia quizzes, computer games), serial storytelling (comics, soap opera, Victorian novels), and so on.

Peters also says that the notion of a "medium" is a trap because it leads us toward "*misplaced abstraction*," the opposite tendency of "*misplaced concreteness.*" If at times we focus too much on the physical medium, at other times our discussions are too concerned with our fantasies about the medium. For example, "broadcasting" became the express purpose of American radio in the 1920s, but what was this new thing called "broadcasting?" The policymakers envisioned radio (and, later, television) as a very different activity than point-to-point conversations between radio amateurs or people speaking on the telephone. Broadcasting was few-to-many. Anyone had who had access to a receiver could listen (and, later, watch), thus creating a large, undifferentiated audience. Viewed in this way, broadcasting could not be democratic. Policymakers guarded access to this mass audience; the limited resource of broadcasting transmission must be given only to a few trustworthy voices who could be regulated (such as corporate radio networks).

Radio stations, therefore, were made responsible for the content of their broadcast messages, unlike "common carriers" such as the mail or telephone systems. The post office or a telephone company is responsible for getting a message from one point to another, but the mail carrier or phone operator is not required to control what is said in a letter or a telephone call. Those letters and telephone calls are private and must not be tampered with. For a government official to listen to a telephone call requires a court warrant, unlike broadcast radio and television messages, which are envisioned as "one size fits all." Our fantasy of "broadcasting" (as opposed to a "common carrier" such as the mail service) governed the way radio developed, instead of the radio medium shaping our notion of broadcasting.

Viewing radio and television as "broadcasting" encourages us to overlook the times that the media function more as point-to-point communication (for instance, when a radio DJ passes along a song dedication from one lover to another) or as few-to-few communication (niche marketing). Thinking of television as a domestic medium ignores the way we use television in public places (such as sports bars). Policymakers continue to understand the telephone as a common carrier, even though the cellular phone has become an entertainment platform for gaming, video, and web applications. Telephone companies accumulate detailed information about a person's cell phone habits (much more specific data than cable and web companies can gather about TV/computer usage, since TV sets and computers cannot differentiate which family member is using the technology within a household, while cell phones are used by individuals). These data, because they are captured on a phone, are private and cannot be sold to advertisers, while web use metrics and TV ratings can be packaged and marketed. The difference between the two systems has less to do with actual content (since the same music video can be downloaded onto a phone or seen on cable television) and more to do with the broad conceptions of what a "telephone" and a "broadcast" are.

Sometimes our fantasies of what a medium is can be traced to the past; at other times, they have more to do with our visions of the medium's future. Often we talk about the "potential" of a medium so vividly that this can obstruct our view of the medium's present. We typically project our society's fears and dreams onto new media, seeing them as roads to utopia or paths to hell. Marketers refer to "virtual reality" as if it existed in today's computer games, and if we uncritically reiterate this idea, this makes it more difficult to see *Second Life* or *Grand Theft Auto* for what they really are. (For more about the hype of "interactive" new media, see Chapter 8.) Games do not present a "world" so convincing that we are truly tempted to forsake the real world and live in an alternate universe. They show us blatantly unrealistic avatars on two-dimensional screens that we control by repeatedly mashing little buttons. This is far from the visions of "virtual reality" presented in *The Matrix* or *The Truman Show*. These films present vivid, popular fears of where new media might take us: a future where the media are so compelling that they blot out the real world. We wonder if media are going to be so omnipresent that we are all participating in a "reality TV" show where no one can tell what is real anymore.

Alternatively, we see technology as opening up the potential for utopia. If everyone is connected online 24 hours a day, we will never have to be alone, according to commercial visions. Goods can flow freely from any single place in the world to another. Rather than depending on powerful gatekeepers (the biased press, Hollywood executives) to choose what we will see and hear, the digital revolution will give voice to a broad range of the disempowered (including under-grad students without rich parents). Instead of having corrupt govern-ment representatives making decisions for us, we can have true democracy, with people voting on a wide range of issues as quickly and easily as taking an online poll. We will live in what Marshall McLuhan called a "global village." Such pipedreams are enticing, but they emphasize the potential over the actual. They ignore roles that power and money continue to play in human relations. Yes, one can download music from obscure bands recorded on the other side of the world, but mass marketing still emphasizes a relative handful of musical artists. As more and more people make videos with digital home equipment, this encourages Hollywood to distinguish its product by concentrating on films that ordinary people cannot make: expensive special-effects-driven blockbusters.

New media do not have capacities for liberation built somewhere into their hardware, nor do they necessarily put us on a slippery slope toward doom. As we have seen in this chapter, predicting the future of any medium is incredibly difficult, given the complicated nature of its development. New media do not have the magical capacity to tear down the structures built by power, but neither are these technologies neces-sarily used as tools of domination over a gullible population. Various interests in our society struggle over what the media mean and what purposes they will serve. By referring to our conceptions of media as "fantasies," I do not mean to imply that these ideas are not important. Fantasies are powerful; they influence us as we try either to move the present world closer to those utopian visions or to steer away from ruin. In this sense, "freedom" and "justice" are unattainable fantasies, but that does not mean that these ideals do not shape our lives.

Our fantasies about media are important, but I believe that in our discussions we should guard against letting our past and future fantasies of media (our "misplaced abstraction") take the place of the actual media in the present. Some people fear that media may be loos-ening our grounding in reality, and films such as *The Matrix* depend on such fears. Although *The Matrix* and *Grand Theft Auto* may be capti-vating, exciting experiences, we also need to recognize that most of us do a perfectly fine job of negotiating the real world once we finish watching/playing. We need not mistake the fantasy of *The Matrix* for the real world.

The medium as virtual machine

One possible way out of the traps of misplaced abstraction and misplaced concreteness is to think of the medium as something more than the technology. Jean-Louis Baudry makes this point when he describes the *"cinematic apparatus"* as involving more than just the mechanical technology of film. In order for "cinema" to occur, for Baudry, there must be cameras, projectors, and film, of course, but the cinematic apparatus involves more than these. The cinema requires the spectator who actively makes sense out of the images on the screen (for more on the spectator, see Chapter 3). The film does not interpret itself; even the most uninspired film requires our participation to piece it together mentally. Without us, the machine of the cinema doesn't work.

In addition, the cinematic apparatus also includes the standard conditions for viewing a film. The movie theater is dark, and the screen is large. You are expected to sit in your seat and be quiet. Everything about this physical situation encourages you to become immersed in the story world unfolding on the screen. Without these conditions, we would not have "cinema." In fact, if you alter those conditions, you have a different "machine." Therefore, part of what makes the apparatus of "television" different is that its images are usually seen under different viewing conditions. The image is smaller, and the room is not completely darkened. People are free to walk around and talk during the program. This encourages a different style of viewer interaction, according to these theories. Instead of gazing at the movie screen, we tend to glance at the television screen in a more interrupted fashion, according to John Ellis.

Years ago when Baudry wrote about the cinematic apparatus and Ellis wrote about television's glance, film and television were very different things seen in very different environments. With the advent of home theaters that play movies on high definition screens with surround sound (and the screening of commercials in theaters), the line between the apparatus of "cinema" and "television" is less clear today. Baudry's ideas can still help us to pry the notion of the "medium" away from the literal machinery. People who have expensive home theater installations often watch movies in fairly "cinematic" conditions (no talking, no moving around, watching in the dark), and so this configuration may come closer to duplicating the cinematic apparatus than the televisual. The technology (video, not film) may not define the "medium" in this case; the viewing conditions may be the stronger factor.

If we expand the notion of medium to describe a particular combination of technology, text, user, and conditions of use, then we can think of "television" as several different apparatuses. One might be the home theater viewing situation with an uninterrupted film/television program; another might be watching commercial television on the same big screen with the lights on and with verbal interaction. These same situations with a smaller television screen would create different apparatuses, as would watching a television program on a laptop. If the actual technology is only part of the definition of a medium, then you overcome the problem of misplaced concreteness.

Other theorists have moved further away from the idea that the technology defines the medium. Wiebe Bijker's book *Of Bicycles, Bakelites, and Bulbs* argues our understanding of a machine is shaped more by how people *use* that machine than by the actual technology. Bijker uses a simple example (the bicycle) to establish his counterintuitive argument. Everyone knows what a bike is: a two-wheeled, self-propelled, people-carrying machine. Bijker argues that the bicycle has been several different "machines" over history, each one with a different social purpose. He traces the bike's history from a "running machine" (which people propelled by putting their feet on the ground) to the "Ordinary bicycle" (an accident-prone machine with one large and one small wheel) to the "safety bicycle" (the more modern bike, with two same-sized wheels, inflatable tires, and a chain). Although these are all bicycles, they were used by different groups of people in different ways. The bicycle began as a sport machine used by young, daring male athletes; this was what Bijker calls the "Macho Bicycle." Non-bikers saw the machine as dangerous, and so their views become relevant because they legally restricted the new mechanical menace. They looked at the same bicycle that the athletes were riding and saw an "Unsafe Bicycle." Manufacturers seeking to overcome these dangers and to increase their customer base tried a range of solutions before settling on the modern "Safety Bicycle," which could be ridden by older men, women, and children.

Bijker asserts that we tend to smooth over history when we look backwards; looking from today's perspective, we see a long steady evolution, arriving at the modern bicycle. Bijker's antidote to this way of thinking involves treating the bicycle as an "artifact" that cannot be classified until we observe how social groups see that artifact. Since this artifact is different things to different portions of society, we should see these as different machines, even if groups are looking at exactly the same technology (the Macho Bicycle and the Unsafe Bicycle). Bijker asserts that technology alone does not define a machine; the social understanding of that machine is also part of its basic definition.

From this perspective, the internet is not an individual thing but is several different media, depending on how people use it. For some it is a mailbox; for others it may be a forum for distributing podcasts, a radio receiver, a television set, a newspaper, a discussion salon, a gaming platform, a telephone, an archive, a searchable database, a store, a recommendation engine, a birthday reminder, a publishing venue, an encyclopedia, and both a community and the source of the destruction of community. If the definition of a medium depends both on hardware and on the way that various groups see that machine, then a medium is as much a social phenomenon as it is a technical one.

Lev Manovich argues that a medium is a set of relationships among communicators. A "medium" is born at a particular moment in history and is created for a particular hardware configuration, but once the medium becomes familiar, it can migrate from its original machinery. For instance, "cinema" became defined as a stream of uninterrupted images on a screen for an audience to see/hear without them affecting the sequence of those images. Cinema took this form for various historical reasons, including technical, social, governmental, and industrial factors. Once we had this conception of cinema, however, we no longer needed cinema to occur on its original hardware (celluloid moving through a projector). "Cinema" (according to Manovich) became something that could happen on a variety of hardware. "Cinema" happens briefly when a cutscene during a game places you in a position of watching characters interact without being able to alter their interactions. It happens when you download movies to your computer screen or when you watch them on your television or iPod. "Radio" becomes a succession of musical numbers heard with minimal or no interaction from the listener (who may be hearing radio waves decoded by a traditional receiver, a satellite signal, or a streaming channel on the internet). A "telephone" call is a relatively private back-and-forth voice conversation between selected people at a limited number of mechanical devices. Although our understanding of a telephone call was forged on technology involving physical wires and bulky receiving/transmitting devices, the phone call now exists independently of its technical origins. A "call" can happen on a desktop computer, a Bluetooth, or a cell phone. For Manovich, a medium is born as hardware but then it becomes a socially recognizable set of communication relations that software can duplicate in many different venues.

We have come a long way from where we started this chapter, when we pointed to a television set and called it "television." We have considered the idea that an "invention" may not be solely based on technology, and we have discussed the power of our fantasies about a medium's essence. I have suggested that groups can look at the same piece of technology and see different "machines." I have proposed that a medium may be created by a set of historical circumstances but afterwards it exists virtually, independent of its technology. This may feel like an academic word game ("Why can't academics just give a simple answer to a simple question?"), but remember that labels have power. When we talk about "television" in a classroom, at a party, or on the floor of the legislature, we are using labels to simplify the discussion. When a slogan asserts, "It's not TV—it's HBO," the network is relying on a specific shared understanding of what we call "TV." We legislate based on these shared labels, but then the resulting laws are implemented on the actual physical media. Definitions of media are important because these "fantasies" have real-life consequences.

Bibliography

Baudry, J.-L. (1986) "Ideological Effects of the Basic Cinematographic Apparatus," in P. Rosen (ed.) *Narrative, Apparatus, Ideology*, New York: Columbia University Press.

Bijker, W. (1995) *Of Bicycles, Bakelites, and Bulbs: Toward a Theory of Sociotechnical Change*, Cambridge, MA: MIT Press.

Bolter, J.D. and Grusin, R. (1999) *Remediation: Understanding New Media*, Cambridge, MA: MIT Press.

Carroll, N. (1988) "The Specificity Thesis," in *Philosophical Problems of Classical Film Theory*, Princeton: Princeton University Press.

Cartier-Bresson, H. (1952) *The Decisive Moment*, New York: Simon and Schuster.

DuGay, P., Hall, S., Janes, L., Mackay, H., and Negus, K. (1997) *Doing Cultural Studies: The Story of the Sony Walkman*, London: Sage.

Ellis, J. (1982) *Visible Fictions*, London: Routledge.

McLuhan, M. (1964) *Understanding Media: The Extensions of Man*, New York: McGraw Hill.

Manovich, L. (2001) *The Language of New Media*, Cambridge, MA: MIT Press.

Peters, J.D. (1994) "The Gaps of Which Communication Is Made," *Critical Studies in Mass Communication* 11.2: 117–40.

Williams, R. (1975) *Television: Technology and Cultural Form*, New York: Schocken Books.

Winston, B. (1998) *Media, Technology, and Society: A History from the Telegraph to the Internet*, New York: Routledge.

Chapter 8

What is interactivity?

"Interactivity" is what makes "new" media "new," or so we are told. What distinguishes computer games, social networking websites, cell phone applications, blogs, and wikis from old media (such as books, film, and television) is that there is some sort of deeper interconnection/ interchange between users and technology. This different quality (whatever it is) is packaged and sold to create new markets and to provide those markets with products. Everyone appears to know what "interactive" means, and yet this defining characteristic of new media seems to have no central definition. It is both a future goal for media to achieve someday and a description of applications as they exist today. "Interactivity" seems like the Supreme Court's description of pornography: I know it when I see it.

In this chapter I will articulate some of the many things that are meant by the word "interactive" today. By becoming more precise about the components of interactivity, I hope to demystify the term a bit. Some of the qualities we value as interactive are not particularly new, although commercial publicity may portray new media as "ground-breaking." Consumers should always be a bit suspicious of sales pitches, and one antidote to commercial exaggeration is the ability to see more clearly what a media product actually does. If our understanding of interactivity remains vague, then we tend to reiterate commercial claims about what is "new and improved" about new media. If we can describe interactivity more specifically, this helps us see the continuities between older and newer media, which may help us discover what is actually "new" about today's media.

I do not think it is particularly useful to separate media into two big piles: those that are interactive and those that are not. In this chapter I will encourage you to ask: in what *ways* is a particular piece of media interactive? Interactivity is not one thing, even though we use a single word to describe it. Nor is it particularly helpful to think of a specific piece of media as having the same kind of interactivity consistently throughout. Media tend to shift in and out of different forms of inter-activity. When you play a computer game, one minute you may be twist-ing the controller as you furiously fight aliens and the next minute you may be sitting idly as you watch characters in a cutscene exchange dia-logue (much like watching a film scene). If we label an entire game "interactive," then we may miss how the game morphs into different forms from moment to moment. Vague discussions of interactivity may interfere with our ability to see new media for what they really are.

Putting interactivity in context

Our society's concept of interactivity may have as much to do with our talk about new media as with the actual media themselves. Interactivity is in the process of being defined as we use the word in our daily lives, and so our understanding of the term changes over time. Playing a new computer game or trying the latest social networking application helps you refine your own expectations of what is "interactive." Customers buying and using software and hardware, mass media writers (and academics) describing these products, and designers creating these environments all contribute to our current understanding of the word.

Since the term has been used by commercial interests to describe a wide range of media, it may be easier to describe what is *not* interactive than to describe what is. As we discussed in Chapter 6, we define something by noting how it is different from other things. Our discus-sion of interactivity begins, then, not by emphasizing any innate qualities of media but by placing the concept in its broader social context.

We can understand interactivity as a criticism of the perceived short-comings of the twentieth century's dominant media: film and television. Inter*activity* is obviously meant to be different from *passive* ways of receiving media, and so this word continues a long discussion about the *"passive" film and television watcher*. The concept of passive viewing suggests that you don't have to do that much when you watch film/TV. You sit back in your recliner/theater seat and let the sea of images and sounds wash over you. The TV couch potato or the film viewer doesn't have to do much except stay awake in order to keep up with what's going on onscreen, according to this way of thinking. The movie or television program continues regardless of whether you are conscious and alert or dozing in your seat, so how interactive can it be?

This understanding of TV and film is part of their appeal. If you want "mindless entertainment" at the end of a hard day's work, then television (understood as a passive form) can provide the goods.

Similarly, much of the appeal of many current Hollywood blockbusters is the pleasure of letting the movie take you on a "rollercoaster ride." You are strapped in and propelled through the story without much control over what will happen, which can provide thrills without seeming to require much activity on your part.

But if we see popular film and television as essentially passive, this encourages us to judge them harshly. In a culture that values action, we tend to look down on passivity. Watching hours and hours of television is something that many of us do, but a passive conception of television gives the medium the sense of being a guilty pleasure. We know that we really should be *doing* something, and since television watching is obviously "doing nothing," it must be a waste of time.

Although many in our society think of film and television as essentially passive media, decades of writing by media studies scholars have overturned this idea in academia. There are no such things as passive media, scholars assert, and that is the position taken by this book. The central component of any medium is you. Movies and television do not come to you predigested; it is up to you to make meanings out of the images and sounds you are given, and that meaning-making process is an active one.

As discussed in Chapter 3, media require us to complete them, and their power comes from involving us in the process. Based on a few cues (a smiling baby, for example), we summon a whole host of associated ideas (innocence, helplessness, and so on) to make sense out of what we see. We participate in film/TV narratives by asking what will happen next, by making predictions and watching to see if our expectations are met. A viewer who hypothesizes, observes, and revises her predictions seems much more active than outward appearances might lead us to believe.

Media scholarship has begun to emphasize the enormous range of meanings that actual viewers make while watching film and television. Viewers and fans also do many different things with films and TV programs rather than just watch them from beginning to end, particularly if they take advantage of technology. People watch videos and turn them off before the ending. They rewind horror DVDs and watch the gory sections over and over again. They record *The Simpsons* on their DVRs and watch portions in slow motion to look for jokes hidden among the images. They turn the sound down on *The Wizard of Oz* and play Pink Floyd's *Dark Side of the Moon* as a substitute soundtrack. Fans intercut Kirk's and Spock's lines from *Star Trek* to create a homosexual romantic scene. They mash up favorite films and television programs (from *The Lord of the Rings* to *Saved by the Bell*) into parodies of *Brokeback Mountain* to post on YouTube. Not only do people actively make meaning from media, but they also interact with older media in quite complicated ways to make new reshaped combinations. As we pay more attention to what actual fans do with media, we realize just how "interactive" film and television can be.

I believe it is useful to differentiate between *the kinds of things people do with media* and *the kind of activities a medium seems to encourage.* When you watch network television, it is clear what kind of viewing is promoted: a viewer who keeps watching the same channel, lured away from the remote control button by neverending promises of what's "coming up next." Similarly, a film in a theater clearly announces how it should be watched: You should stay in your seat without smoking or loud talking. These *meta-messages* communicate to our society a particular vision of how film and television work, and these messages powerfully shape how we think about those media. A film announces that you should be physically and verbally passive when you watch it, and this influences the way we think about the movies.

So why do these meta-messages about how to watch film and television programs matter? After all, real viewers frequently do things with media that they are not "supposed" to do. People do talk and move around in a movie theater, and they do channel surf through their cable systems, even though the channels encourage us to stay tuned. When I discuss with my students the practice of editing together a Spock and Kirk romance, inevitably one of them will say something like, "But the creators never intended that to happen." And that student is quite right. When we watch media, we also gain a sense of what we're "intended" to do with that text, and undoubtedly certain fan interactions violate those suggestions of what we're "supposed" to do with the episodes. At the meta-level it's clear that we're "supposed" to watch a horror video from beginning to end, although in practice actual viewers can fast-forward to the "good parts."

When we generally discuss film and television in our society, we tend to think about the meta-messages. We usually discuss film/TV as they are "supposed" to be watched, not as they are actually watched. We think of these older media as passive, although real-world viewers and fans do much more interesting things with them. We tend to think that most people watch film and television as they're supposed to do (passively receiving messages), although *we* are savvier than those dupes. Or perhaps "deviant" fans who need to "get a life" spend their time actively making mashups, while most others watch film and TV as we "should."

When we discuss media (new or old), we tend to reduce them to the minimum activities that they appear to require. Film and TV appear to require almost no effort, and so this is how we envision them. We do not tend to see media as providing us with material that we can use in different ways. Instead of thinking of media as providing opportunities for us to reshape images (either in our minds or by creating new media), we think of older media as following the meta-messages that we should view them passively.

Interactive media are clearly *not* like television and film, understood in this way. They do not proceed if the user dozes in his/her chair. They require physical and mental action from the viewer in order to proceed. Unlike film and television, many computer games come to an end if the player stops moving the controller for a long time. They require constant participation by the player, either at blitzkrieg speed or at a more deliberative pace.

Another significant context for understanding interactivity is our society's emphasis on "*control*" and the mass media. When we discuss the effects of television violence on children, or subliminal advertising, or media-related stalkings, we assume television can influence behavior, often making people more antisocial (see Chapter 6 for a fuller discussion). In these conversations television is a medium that is (at least) outside of our control and (at most) a medium that can control people, particularly the unstable or the gullible.

Interactive media revel in the fact that you, the user, are in control. You can travel to any virtual space you want in *World of Warcraft*. You can stay there as long as you want, doing whatever you choose to do, according to the ideal conceptualization of interactive media. You are behind the controls of the car of your choice in a racing game such as *Forza Motorsport*, and so your commands propel you around the racetrack. In strategy games such as *Civilization*, you can have God-like powers to create natural disasters and wipe cities off the map. Computer games often offer the fantasy of extending our control to technology that far exceeds most of our real grasps: jumbo jets, pricey sports cars, interstellar cruisers, and BFGs (Big F***ing Guns). They can offer a simulated feel for what it must be like to have control over a superbly trained body, such as a black belt karate fighter. The interactive game promises the fantasy of control over an entire world.

This emphasis on the power of control tends to ignore just how dull and frustrating it can be to control an onscreen character. If they are unfamiliar with a game space, players can spend a considerable amount of time moving from room to room without really doing anything except bumping into walls. If you were watching a movie where a character did that, chances are you would walk out of the theater. The power fantasy of control encourages us to downplay the downside of actual game play: boredom and frustration.

Such fantasies rely on central values of our hyper-capitalist society, such as "*choice*." We perceive that "choice" is a good thing, allowing us to exercise our freedoms. The concept of democracy enshrines choice as a basic principle, and capitalism has refined this rhetoric to make choice a fundamental principle of business. We need relatively free markets so that increased competition can provide more choices for the consumer (and more choice is necessarily better, in this way of thinking).

Commercial media also use the rhetoric of choice to sell their wares. Cable television, for instance, rose to prominence largely based on this appeal: more channels, more choices, therefore better TV. And yet new media differentiate themselves from television by emphasizing choice. Television only offers the choice among different channels, but the activity remains the same: passive watching. Television may offer you 1,000 channels, but often the viewer finds there's "nothing on." Although cable systems emphasize the number of choices they present to viewers, new media implicitly criticize this kind of choice as being too limited, too monotonous.

The fantasy of interactivity offers a choice of different kinds of activities, not just one (watching). Interactive players can run, leap, punch, drive, fly, swim, shoot, and screw within the virtual worlds of the computer games. Players have choices about where they travel within those worlds as well as choices about what they do when they get there. But there is a bit of slippage in this way of talking about players' activity. It is our avatar (our ambassador to the virtual world) who runs, leaps, punches, and so on; we, the actual players, are only moving a small piece of technology.

The *physical action* required for most games is small (pressing buttons on an Xbox controller or moving a Wii wand) but significant in the context of the "*couch potato*." We can easily assume that the couch potato's mental inactivity matches his/her lack of physical activity, leading us to judge this figure harshly. The fantasy of interactivity portrays the player as more mentally active than the couch potato, and even the slightest degree of added movement can be read as a signal that we are progressing away from the couch potato syndrome. Parents who dislike computer games in general may approve of *Dance Dance Revolution*, *Rock Band*, or Wii because these gamers are now at least moving. Yet few parents complain about the inactivity of their children when they read.

Discussing "activity" or "interactivity" often blurs the physical with the mental, both of which have complicated places in our values system. We assign different social importance to different kinds of knowledge, and we make judgments accordingly. The academic knowledge required to do well on *Jeopardy* is valued more than the shopping savvy needed to succeed on *The Price Is Right*, and so *Jeopardy*'s social position is more "highbrow." It is more socially acceptable to say one watches *Jeopardy*, while *The Price Is Right* tends to be more of a guilty pleasure. This difference in "brow level" can conceal how the "game engine" of both shows is roughly the same. Both shows encourage viewers to interact with the television, to play along by shouting answers at the contestants. The interactivity of both is similar, though our cultural assumptions encourage us to see *Jeopardy* as more mentally involving. Similarly, our culture tends to situate violence as being more lowbrow, and so first-person shooter games have a more denigrated reputation than puzzle games. When someone wants to discuss the horrors of computer games, they will gravitate toward *Grand Theft Auto*, not *Peggle*, although various versions of *Grand Theft Auto* have remarkably complex storylines that echo plotlines from the critically acclaimed *The Sopranos*. One complicating factor in discussing "activity" and "interactivity" is the *highbrow/lowbrow status of the media's content*. "Passive media" seem to be most troubling to our society when they present lowbrow material.

Our society puts a particular value on "imagination," but when dealing with media it particularly seems to value our *ability to imagine spaces*. One of the alleged advantages of books is that each of us can imagine our own version of what Harry Potter and Hogwarts look like, which is a powerful interaction between our minds and the words on the page. People made a similar argument about the power of old-time network radio such as *The Jack Benny Show* and Orson Welles's version of *The War of the Worlds*. Because people staged the action in their heads, radio dramas and comedies seemed more participatory. Television and film, on the other hand, stage action visually. These media seem to do the work of spatial imagination for us, substituting a particular version of Harry Potter and Hogwarts for our multiple mental versions. To this way of thinking, reading in generally is better for you than watching film and television because books give free rein to our spatial imagination.

However, this places value only on a particular form of imagination. What about the process of predicting what will happen next in a film/television narrative? Why isn't the activity of making story hypotheses and revising them as you get new information just as "imaginative" as picturing a space? Of course, both processes are "interactive" and "imaginative" in different ways, though society rarely sees these mental media processes as equally valuable.

Let's summarize what we've covered so far about the way society talks about media, interactivity, and values. Interactivity becomes a selling point by appearing to offer something different than older, more "passive" media such as film and television do. Film and television allow us to "visit" new worlds and see through other people's eyes, but interactive computer games present us with the fantasy of controlling a character or even the whole world. Once our avatar is in the game world, interactivity offers that onscreen body "choices," taking advantage of our society's notion that choice in general is a good thing (even when the choices are fairly dull). The new media sales pitch appears to offer choice, control, and interactivity as radically new qualities, without recognizing continuities with older media. Such PR tends to reduce film and television to the apparent minimum effort required by those media. They confuse the meta-messages about how we should watch film/TV with the more complicated activities that real viewers do. They confuse the relative physical inactivity of the "couch potato" with mental inactivity, ignoring the imagination and participation required to make sense out of visual storytelling. Our society's preference for highbrow knowledge and spatial imagination further clouds our ability to recognize interactivity across various media. We need a more precise way to discuss interactivity that cuts through the vague, value-laden language.

Strongly and weakly designed mediaspaces

Obviously not all new media are the same. There are differences between the interactivity of a computer game and that of a blog or a chat room. I will begin by drawing a very broad distinction between what I call "strongly designed" and "weakly designed" mediaspaces.[1] A strongly designed mediaspace has been authored and constructed to provide different audience members with similar experiences. People interact with *Halo* in order to experience the particular blend of violence and mayhem designed into the *Halo* universe, and we watch and rewatch *The Big Lebowski* to enjoy hanging out with the Dude. Films, television programs, and many computer games are strongly designed by a few people to be experienced by many, and these few-to-many media bear the imprints of their creators. Although games are sometimes

1 This distinction between strongly and weakly designed (along with other terms in this chapter) is adapted from G.M. Smith (1999) "A Few Words about Interactivity," in *On a Silver Platter: CD-ROMs and the Promises of a New Technology*, New York: New York University Press.

described as "virtual reality," they are much more highly shaped by human intent than any real world. Strongly designed mediaspaces are personalized worlds that try to provide heightened experiences. They can be compelling because their worlds have been shaped and designed to provide significant payoffs for our time investment.

Of course chat facilities and blogs are purposefully designed, too. However, they are not *strongly* designed. People do not "visit" a chat space to experience a cleverly designed universe. They use chat rooms as a neutral space to "meet" other people; they blog to exchange ideas with those interested in similar topics. The appeal of a chat room is not in the "room" itself but in the discussions you have with people who share your interests. The space itself is not compelling, although the conversations one has in it may be.

To use a metaphor, the difference between strongly and weakly designed mediaspaces resembles the difference between entering a furnished house and an unfurnished one. When you enter a furnished house, you react to the spatial design and decorations, which bear the imprint of the owner's tastes. The furnishings tell us what activities are expected in those rooms; clearly the bedroom is for sleeping and the dining room is for eating. When you enter an unfurnished house, you get more of a sense of the space's possibilities. A particular room might be a used as either a bedroom or a dining room, and the house's overall feel is only broadly defined by the architectural design. The pleasures of an unfurnished room lie in its possibilities; the pleasures of a furnished room reside in the sense of an already actualized design concept.

The furor over "interactivity" has often emphasized the "do it yourself" possibilities of future media. What fun it will be to create our own stories, bend narratives to our will, to wield a creator's power over a virtual world! And yet it is hard to imagine such DIY narration ever entirely replacing the experience of a well-authored universe, primarily because it's just damn hard to create a compelling world. We go to strongly designed mediaspaces such as computer games, movies, and television programs because we want to experience a story/world that has been well made for our consumption. We may enjoy holding up our end of an online conversation, but that also requires considerable mental and social effort. Strongly designed mediaspaces lure us with the promise of experiencing a more interesting virtual world than we could design ourselves. Just as inexpensive home video equipment did not destroy the Hollywood video market, just as the relative ease of writing on a word processor did not create a surge of new novelists, the ability to "do it yourself" will not replace the desire to experience a universe that has already been well made for you. In spite of the growth of other kinds of interactive experiences, there will always be a market for the strongly designed mediaspace.

The weakly designed mediaspace has its appeal as well, as a place where users can "post" their expressions (in print or video or sound format) on a "bulletin board" or blog for all to see; where we can "chat" in a public "room" or via private instant messaging. To call these spaces "weakly designed" does not mean that little thought goes into creating a social networking site. In fact, small differences in design can make a big difference in use. For example, the advantage of Twitter is its design limitation. By restricting user posts to 140 characters, Twitter seems to invite participation that does not require much effort, making posting a more spontaneous, "in the moment" form of interactivity. Design choices such as these do make a difference, but a weakly designed mediaspace focuses on its participants, not the designers. Your choice of whether to participate in Facebook, MySpace, or Twitter probably has more to do with the people on that particular social network, though certainly the "look" and function of a site have ramifications. Your decision to follow a blog depends more on your personal interests than on the page layout.

The structural frameworks of weakly designed mediaspaces vary based on *timing* and *access*. Blogs and social network status updates function like "bulletin boards": users post their words or videos so that they may be seen publicly at any time. Instant messaging (using voice, video, or text) is a real-time exchange, and so chat room sessions or Skype conversations or cell phone texting are more immediate and evanescent. Many large sites contain both kinds of mediaspaces. For instance, you can update your public status on your Facebook "wall," or you can engage in private real-time chat. Access to these spaces varies from one-on-one text messaging to private networks of "friends" to anyone with a web browser. Of course one form of interaction may be recirculated in another form. A private text conversation or webcam interaction can be recorded and posted for broader consumption, much to your embarrassment. And media technologies, when placed in actual users' hands, can blur the boundaries between these mediaspaces. "Viral videos," for example, can seem more personally targeted than a mere posting on a bulletin board such as YouTube. They become "push" technology instead of requiring users to "pull" the video from the site.

Thinking of mediaspaces as weakly designed allows us to find continuities with computer programs that are not often seen as "interactive," such as spreadsheet or word processing software. A spreadsheet is clearly "interactive," when you think about it: You enter numbers into the spreadsheet, and the program performs functions on the data.

Although you may prefer one spreadsheet program over another, a spreadsheet's value is in its content, not its authored "feel." Most spreadsheets and documents have very limited access; often they are privately held on your own personal computer. But if you open up the access to a document to more people, you create a weakly designed interactive mediaspace. A wiki (such as Wikipedia) is primarily a database engine that is transformed into a more interactive environment by broader access.

In some ways, spreadsheet and word processing software offer more "choice" than graphic-intensive computer games, in that they can produce an infinite number of different documents (as opposed to the relatively limited number of moves available to a player). What these programs gain in flexibility, they lose in a compelling sense of interactivity. This is why database programs are not the first examples of "interactivity" that come to mind, though clearly they function interactively.

The form of weakly designed mediaspaces varies based on timing and access, but the focus remains on user-generated content, not the design of the interactive universe. These are broad distinctions, and users can repurpose mediaspaces for their own aims. Players in a massively multiplayer online roleplaying game (MMORPG) do not necessarily have to fight; they can congregate for real-time conversations that resemble chat more than typical roleplay battles. As always, you cannot predict what real users will do with a technology simply by looking at the technology. But still you can feel the rough distinction between the interactivity encouraged by an MMORPG and a blog. Since the weakly designed mediaspace depends so much on its user-generated content, I will focus the rest of this chapter on discussing the various forms of interactivity in strongly designed mediaspaces.

Interacting with objects

Seeing films, television programs, novels, and computer games as "strongly designed" helps us see the continuities among these media. Rather than thinking of the older media as "linear" and the newer as "nonlinear," I suggest that these media differ in the boundaries they establish for the player's/viewer's/reader's interactions with the strongly designed mediaspaces. In spite of fantasies of "interactivity" giving us infinite freedom of "choice," every media text puts limits on what we, the player/user/viewer, can do. These boundaries powerfully shape the quality of our interactivity with mediaspaces.

Although weakly designed mediaspaces such as chat facilities and bulletin boards emphasize interactivity with other *users*, interactivity in strongly designed mediaspaces is better thought of as interaction with *objects*, not with people. This notion may seem counterintuitive at the start, since our "interactions" with objects in a computer game seem quite one-way. Throwing a rock or wielding a bazooka feels more like an "action" than an interaction, but the objects in a computer game are no ordinary objects. They operate under a basic principle of multimedia/game design: that any object in the space, whether an image of a person or a rock, is potentially capable of an enormous range of responses to our actions. A rock thrown in the real world is propelled through the air toward a target. A rock in a computer game may respond to clicks with a giggle, an explosion, a fart, a trumpet fanfare, or a song and dance. One might predict that "grabbing" the rock might result in hurling it toward a target, but in a strongly designed interactive universe you never know until you try it. Game designers are not bound by the technology to linking rocks to throwing; they can just as easily link rocks to rolls, or rocks to clocks.

Within the world of the designer, this capacity for response is made possible by "object-oriented programming." Designers think of a person's interactions with the computer as a range of possible "events" which occur to "objects" that the designer defines. The designer's job is to associate responses to events. If a user presses a certain controller key when their avatar's hands are near a rock, this is an event that calls for a response by the program. Any response can be linked to any event.

An important part of the definition of an object is specifying the object's boundaries. An object, as defined by the program, need not be exactly the same as an object onscreen. One can make two functional objects (having two separate responses) out of what appears to be a single onscreen object (for instance, one can define controller commands that respond differently when grabbing a box lid than when grabbing the box itself). The fact that that an area appears to be inhabited by a single onscreen object is not crucial. From a player's point-of-view, a game can be inhabited by monsters and warriors; from a designer's point-of-view, it is composed of events and objects. When game designers define objects, they are really defining onscreen areas to respond to specific controller commands.

Object-oriented programming fundamentally reshaped the structure of multimedia spaces. In the real world, we expect that humans have a much wider range of responses to our actions than objects do. If I throw a rock I might hit a window or a police officer, but the rock won't make off-color suggestions or snicker at me. In the real world those capacities belong to humans alone. What object-oriented programming does is to give objects and people/characters in a game a kind of radical equality.

There is no reason why people/characters in a game should be able to snicker and objects should not. After all, both are nothing more than areas defined on the screen. It takes no more effort to make a rock snicker in a game than it does to make a character snicker. Designers can use sophisticated "physics engines" to make game objects simulate real-world motion (with friction and velocity), or they can choose to make the object respond in ways that have little to do with the real world. In an interactive game, characters and physical items are both "objects" that act entirely within the boundaries designed into the game.

The gamer is not concerned with the designer's view of the created world. What matters is the interface, not the processing that goes on behind the scenes. The player is concerned with three factors that shape our interactions with objects in a strongly designed mediaspace. One is: *What can the player do to objects onscreen?* The obvious answer, in most cases, is that all the player can do is click on objects with various buttons on a controller. But games translate the controller commands into different virtual actions. A push of a controller button can change the avatar's tools from a gun to a lockpick. A change of tool changes your capabilities in the virtual world.

In the real world we can use an object in a variety of ways. I can use my hand to grab, to slap, to tickle, and to wave. Even tools that have a seemingly straightforward purpose (such as a hammer) are not limited to their primary use. For instance, in the real world I can use a hammer as a paperweight. But in the game world our range of possible actions toward objects is more limited. Although you can use a match to light a virtual fire, you may not be able to use it to clean your virtual teeth. These are authored, purposeful objects, and the quality of interactivity depends on the possible actions we can perform on objects.

What can the object do to respond to our actions? Since an interactive authored object, unlike a real-world object, is potentially capable of an extraordinary range of responses, which one(s) actually make up an object's reaction? Are they predictable (does the monster explode each time I fire at it?), or do they vary depending on the situation? How many possible responses does an object have? Objects may respond differently to your avatar depending on your avatar's current status in the game. The interactivity in a game such as *Scribblenauts* depends on reconceptualizing the world as full of useful, surprising objects from dry-erase markers to dung. How constrained are the responses from these game objects?

The third factor in discussing interactivity with objects is: *What can these objects do to us (or our avatar) without our prompting?* Can they initiate an interaction? Can they prompt us to make a response? Can a monster attack us, or do we have to seek it out? A shoot-'em-up game such as *Half-Life 2* depends on an enormous number of objects which initiate attacks on us. In a game such as *Grim Fandango*, objects rarely demand such immediate attention; instead, we have to search them out for interaction.

The balance of these three factors determines much about the nature of the interaction we have with the interactive game. Does the game depend mostly on our finding the correct actions to drive the program and achieve the goals set for a game level? Does the pleasure of playing the game come largely from the interesting responses we get to our actions? Is the game driven by actions initiated by the program, demanding our response? The game then can set up a cyclical interaction: our action, the game's reaction, the game's instigating action, our reaction to it, and so on. Or the game can deemphasize one portion of the cycle. For instance, some interactive media depend on the action–response cycle (you press buttons, it responds), rather than initiating an action without our bidding. Due to the mixed nature of multimedia, strongly designed mediaspaces sometimes switch among different interactive modes.

The *initial unpredictability of interactive objects* is the first fundamental that shapes the quality of our interactions with games. The other fundamental interactive possibility is the ability to *interact with the narration*. Narration is the way the story (the narrative) is told. A particular story can be told with a variety of possible narrations. Two different stage productions of a play can present different narrational strategies in interpreting the same text. Different viewpoints, or order of presenting events, tones, and emphases in narration make for a different experience of the story.

The possibility of interacting with the narration creates infinitely more complexity. Not only can the same story be told in different ways, but interactivity presents the added possibility of changing the story itself. Interactivity with the narration implies more than just reinterpreting the same narrative; it also brings the possibility of new and different story events. Interacting with the narration allows games to reshape the events that make up the story.

Interaction with the narration can take several forms in games. First, games can provide several different *perspectives on the action*. For the film and television director presenting a scene, the choice of which camera angles to use and what order to present them in is a matter of controlling information to the audience. Do we get to see the ticking bomb under the table, or does the film withhold this information? How early in the scene should the audience discover the hidden bomb? Do we see one actor's frightened face but not another's? Whenever a director/editor/cinematographer chooses one perspective over another, this influences what information an audience has and when it has it. Giving and withholding information powerfully alters the emotional appeal of a film or television program.

When a computer game gives us a broad range of choices in viewing a scene, it relinquishes tight control of one key variable in evoking our emotions. It replaces this by giving us the pleasure of being the "director," of choosing the "camera" position that shows us the action. Games such as *Fallout 3* offer us the opportunity to swing our perspective above, below, and behind our avatar using a "free camera." And yet games sometimes constrain our perspective when they show a cutscene of dialogue between characters. When they need to convey important story information, games reduce our interactivity of perspective, acknowledging the tight link between perspective and storytelling. In fact, many game designers see themselves as creating *spaces* for users to roam instead of telling *stories*. The designer places boundaries on where and how fast we can move in this space. The game designer, like the film director and editor, must choose which perspectives to allow the player to have. What objects can we move all the way around? Can we look above, below, or inside it? Strongly defined mediaspaces differ in how much interactivity of perspective they provide. If we are given too few choices of perspective, game play "feels" more like the viewpoints have been pre-selected for us (as in a film), instead of allowing us to select them. However, if designers give us too many possible "camera angles" on the action, they potentially sacrifice the narrationally powerful option of withholding information from us. They emphasize the game as space over the game as story.

A second form of narrational interactivity involves *interacting with the series of events*. By "event" I mean a story occurrence which has lasting, irreversible effects on the game. Events change the game's status. Sample events might include solving a puzzle, picking up an object which will be needed later in the game, killing a character, and destroying or building a structure. Simply picking up an object (a wooden stake, for instance) is not necessarily an event; however, picking up and carrying a wooden stake you will need later is a story event. Your capabilities as a player have changed, as you will discover if and when you encounter a vampire.

Narrational interactivity offers the possibility of allowing us to choose which events will be important in our story and in which order we will witness those events. Early "interactive" print books offered the ability to choose which events made up a particular reading of a novel.

Using a tree structure, the book presented a series of decisions for the reader to make, which influenced which events made up the story ("If you want Bill to call for help, go to page 45. If you want him to run away, go to page 61"). Interactivity with events at least opens up the possibility of choosing which events will make up the story.

At present, there are relatively few commercial games that act on the early promise of tree-structure print narratives to allow different events to make up the game's "story." In most games, the player must accomplish *all* narratively significant events. You must collect all the significant objects in a level, or you must successfully navigate all levels of play, or you must visit all important virtual sites. If you leave out any one of these narratively significant events, you cannot win the game (without the help of secret cheat codes). The interactivity of events presented in computer games tends to remain fairly limited, at least in comparison with other earlier interactive texts. The fear seems to be that if designers did not force players to complete all the tasks, the players might miss some of the spaces the designers worked so hard to create, and so they would not get their "full money's worth" for the game. The possibility to choose different narrative events was publicized as an early potential of interactive media, and this possibility seems to be underdeveloped in computer game design.

What games do offer instead is the ability to interact with narration concerning the *sequence* of events. You can drive all over the city in *Grand Theft Auto*, engaging in the mayhem of your choice. If we are required to visit all the sites in a game level before moving on, at least we are able to visit them in an order of our own choosing. Envisioning a game as a "sandbox" for us to explore clearly differentiates these interactive mediaspaces from films and television programs, which clearly specify the order in which we see and hear things.

On first impression this ability to rearrange the sequence of events seems to be one of the primary differences between film/television and games, with games providing almost unlimited freedom to perform actions in the order you want. However, games, like film and television, also restrict and set boundaries on the sequence of actions. Games require us to do certain activities before we are able to do others. Perhaps players can function in a cave only after they have successfully obtained a magic torch, or maybe they can only defeat an intimidating boss after they have accumulated a certain power level.

Such events in computer games tend to be conditional but not chained. A film/television narrative chains together conditional events to create a seemingly airtight sequence. If a man wants to solve his wife's murder, he must find the one-armed killer; to find the one-armed killer, he needs address information on amputees; to find this information, he must break into a hospital; and so on. Each of these events is conditional on previous events, and these events are chained together so that any large failure jeopardizes the overall goal (to find a killer). In a game there may be conditional events (you must find the torch before you can go in the cave), but failing to accomplish any one event does not necessarily bring the whole story to a halt. It merely prevents you from accomplishing the next conditional event. There are usually plenty of things to do in the meantime: other sites to visit, other conditional events to accomplish.

The game does not present infinite freedom to change the sequence of events. In fact, the restrictions that a game places on your ability to change the event sequence are crucial to the quality of the interactivity. More restrictions tend to bind the narration toward a single storyline, and fewer restrictions give a wider horizon of interactivity. The innovation of *Deus Ex* was that the player did not have to visit every space, creating multiple ways to complete the game. *Deus Ex* provided more interaction with the narration, allowing the storyline to branch in ways that resembled earlier "interactive" books. The chain of conditional events is not as restricted as in earlier games, creating a different form of interactivity.

More interactivity is not necessarily a better idea. Restrictions are crucial to create tension or to give a sense of accomplishment. Part of the reason one feels pleasure when unlocking a particular puzzle or defeating a boss within a game is because you know it's not easy. You know that you had to accomplish several other tasks before you solved the puzzle or you had to accumulate enough strength/experience points to defeat this foe, and these conditional events are necessary to provide a sense of achievement. Games tend to balance the emotional payoffs of restricted, conditional events with the freedom to influence the overall sequence of events.

Speed and the impression of choice

Games, then, are strongly designed mediaspaces that allow us to interact with objects (through avatar actions, object responses, and object initiation) and with the narration (through changing perspectives or rearranging event sequences). These two sets of factors determine much of the nature of interactivity with a game. There are two other important factors that affect the quality of our interactions, and these factors are not exclusively narrational or object oriented. These are overarching factors that affect the quality of both our interactivity with objects and our interactivity with the narration.

First is the number of options available to the player at any one time. Current notions of interactivity often depend on the *impression that we have an infinite series of choices* available to us. Early adventure games restricted the player to a few possible movements (up, down, right, left, forward, backward), but much contemporary interactivity gives the impression that we have many possible options at any given time. Of course a game cannot present a truly infinite array of options, but it does not have to. To feel fully interactive in today's world, a game must only convince us that there *seem* to be infinite possibilities for the player's actions.

Most games tend to give a sense of infinite choice by emphasizing our ability to interact with objects in a sequence of our choosing. The *total* number of possible combinations for maneuvering objects and visiting locations seems infinite, thus making computer games seem more interactive than, say, a tree-structure novel. The multiple pathway novel has one kind of interactive advantage (the ability to choose different story events), but it has less of the overarching impression that we have infinite options.

The other overarching factor in interactivity is the frequency of the interaction. Does the game encourage fast-paced interaction, or does it tend to evoke a slower interchange of actions? Thus far our discussion on interactivity has emphasized the kinds of interactions between player and game. The frequency of those interactions can be just as important a factor in the quality of our interactive experience. *Resident Evil 4* offers a relatively limited choice of action: basically we can move in various directions, and we can shoot at zombies using different weapons. However, because the zombies come at us so rapidly, forcing us to respond, the interaction between player and object is highly charged.

Using these concepts, one can begin to describe the nature of interactivity with a game more precisely. *Portal* is a game that restricts your actions to a single tool with a single purpose: a "portal gun" that creates entrances/exits in walls. The game is not dependent on objects initiating interactions with us, nor is the pace of interaction frenzied. Instead we must learn how this world reacts in order to move through the portals correctly. The events are highly contingent. We can move freely through the space in the order we choose, but we can only visit certain spaces once we unlock particular puzzles, and we must accomplish all required tasks in order to complete the game.

Deus Ex, on the other hand, gives you many different tools (from rocket launchers and crowbars to body augmentations) that you can use to interact with the world. Much of the action depends on you reacting to the hosts of terrorists (humanoid and otherwise) who attack you with menacing speed, as many first-person shooter games do. As in many adventure games, we must search out objects to provide clues that solve puzzles, though there are multiple story paths that the player can choose to accomplish the game's goals.

This is by no means a complete description of the games. Certainly there are many factors that contribute to our overall experience of the two games: the moral questions about authority/euthanasia in *Portal* or about humanity/technology in *Deus Ex*, or the unsettling ambient environments of both games. Yet these factors do not contribute to the *interactivity* of these games, though they certainly are important to the pleasure of playing the games. Although interactivity is the hallmark of new media, it is by no means the only pleasure, and in some cases may not even be the primary pleasure. For instance, the lush environments of *Shadow of the Colossus* or *Rez* distinguish these games more than any innovations in their gameplay. The major payoffs of playing computer games can come from their themes, tones, moods, and style. These factors play a large part in the pleasure we gain from a game, although they are not necessarily interactive qualities. To explain a game's interactivity is not to explain the entire game.

Interactivity is only one quality (although an important one) that shapes our experience of new media. As a critical consumer and a media student, you need to be able to separate the hype about interactivity from the structure of mediaspaces, recognizing what pleasures and frustrations come from interactivity and what experiences come from other factors. Learning how to describe the nature of these games' interactivity is a useful starting place for the real work of analysis: examining the details of a specific interactive environment or of the particular interaction between a player/user and a mediaspace.

Further reading

Jenkins, H. (2006) *Convergence Culture: Where Old and New Media Collide*, New York: New York University Press.

Juul, J. (2005) *Half-Real: Video Games between Real Rules and Fictional Worlds*, Cambridge, MA: MIT Press.

Index